LANDSCAPES OF

Mallorca

a countryside guide

Second Edition

Valerie Crespí-Green

SUNFLOWER
BOOKS

First published 1984
This second edition
published 1987 by
Sunflower Books
12 Kendrick Mews
London SW7 3HG, UK

ISBN: 0-948513-25-X

IMPORTANT NOTE TO THE READER

I have tried to ensure that the descriptions and maps in this book are error-free at press date. The book will be up-dated, where necessary, whenever future printings permit. It will be very helpful to me to receive your comments (sent in care of the publishers, please), for the up-dating of future printings.

I also rely on walkers to take along a good supply of common sense — as well as this book — on their rambles. Conditions change fairly quickly on Mallorca: storm damage can make a walk unsafe, or a route currently open to walkers could be enclosed in private land. If a route is not as I outline it, and your way ahead is not secure, return to the point of departure. **Do not attempt to complete a walk under hazardous conditions.** Please read carefully the notes on pages 54 to 63 and make your walks in safety, while at the same time respecting the privacy of Mallorca's farmlands.

Drawings by Katharina Kelly
Maps by Pat Underwood and Katharina Kelly
Photographs by John Underwood
Typeset by Allset Composition, London
Printed and bound in the UK by A Wheaton and Co Ltd, Exeter
BB/BH

⊛ Contents

◉ Preface

When you think of Mallorca, do you imagine a typical holiday island — hotels and souvenir shops strung out along busy esplanades... bars advertising 'English Fish and Chips' and 'Tea Like Mum Makes'... a multitude of night clubs and discos advertising *flamenco* shows on large and gaudy posters? Do you think this is Mallorca?

I hope not.

Of course, the hotel-crowded esplanades *do* exist, but beyond the tourist centres, an exciting and altogether different Mallorca awaits your discovery. And with this new addition to the 'Landscapes' series, I hope to help you to find it.

The book is divided into three main parts — **touring, picnicking** and **walking**, each with its own introduction. *Do* take a look at each introductory section, even if you think it may not apply to your holiday plans. You may find something of interest, because each section of the book has been written with one aim in view — to help you discover the 'hidden' Mallorca that most tourists never see.

Motorists will find that the ten car tours cover more than enough territory for the average visit. The touring map has purposely been kept to a compact, easy-to-use format. It is up-to-date and contains information not found on other maps — for instance, where some roads are now closed to motorists, picnic sites with tables, and the location of walks along the route of your car tour.

Picnickers can travel by private or public transport to all the picnic spots — some of them chosen for their delightful surroundings, others for their far-reaching views. *All* of the picnic spots have one thing in common: you won't have to walk very far from your transport to reach them.

Walkers of all ages and abilities will enjoy discovering the island's hidden landscapes as they cross an incredible variety of terrain — some spectacular, some serene. For beginners, there are easy strolls along flat tracks by the coast (for instance, Walk 23) and others (like Short walk 17) on delightful country lanes. Hardy walkers can tackle more challenging terrain to *miradors* only accessible on foot, and experts can scale mountain peaks or descend into the depths of the Pareis gorge. . . .

Acknowledgements

I am extremely grateful for the invaluable help of the following:

For guiding: Mauricio Espinar, without whose extensive knowledge and experience this book could not have been written.

For permission to adapt their maps: The Servicio Geográfico del Ejercito, Madrid.

For checking the walks: David and Sally Murch, Clive Scott, John and Pat Underwood, George and Mary Clarke, and the many people who have sent me helpful comments since the first edition of the book was published.

Finally, my most grateful thanks also to Maria-José and Francisco Merchán, for their valuable assistance in taking notes and giving me a rest from driving; and special thanks to Sharon Ranero for accompanying me on some of the walks.

Comment

by Air Vice Marshal Sir Bernard Chacksfield, KBE, CB, RAF (Retired); Member World Scout Committee 1972-1978; Chief Commissioner of Scouts for England 1968-1980

Mallorca is world-renowned as an ideal holiday centre, and I personally have enjoyed discovering the island over many years. Sunshine and beaches are the first delights that spring to mind when thinking of the island. Less well known to many visitors is the beauty of the mountains — amongst which are some of the loveliest walks in the world.

Valerie has produced an excellent book, based upon her personal exploration on many walks over the island. It will help walkers, bird-watchers and other lovers of nature to increase their enjoyment of this lovely island and will contribute to the pleasure of *all* holiday-makers who can use it to discover new island landscapes. I can thoroughly recommend it.

☀ Getting about

There is no doubt that a **hired car** is the most convenient way of getting about Mallorca, and car rental on the island is good value. Be sure to 'shop around' amongst the many car-hire firms (where English is spoken generally); the prices can vary by up to perhaps 40 per cent!

The second most flexible form of transport is to hire a **taxi**, and, especially if three or four people are sharing the cost, this becomes an attractive idea. If you're making a taxi journey outside the city centre (an un-metred journey), do agree on the price *before* setting out; all taxi-drivers should carry an official price list.

Coach tours are the most popular way of seeing Mallorca, and veritable convoys of tourist-loaded coaches converge onto the roads during the summer season, much to the frustration of the local drivers (and tourists in hired cars). However, you can get to know the island comfortably in this way, before embarking on your own adventures.

The most economical way of getting about is by local transport — hourly **train** services on the Palma—Inca line; the 'wild-west' **narrow-gauge railway** between Palma and Sóller; the **tram** between Puerto de Sóller and Sóller, and finally the local **bus** network. All these public transport systems are economical, reliable — and much more fun! The Sóller train is one of the island's tourist attractions. But the train between Palma and Inca is also amusing: the run is a flat one across the plain and the train hurtles along like a 'blue bullet'. Remember, too, that you'll have very good views perched up on bus seats, and that generally the buses are new and very comfortable. (Note that, outside Palma, you can flag down a bus anywhere along its route, without making for the centre of a village.)

The following two pages show you where to find your public transport in Palma; other public transport and taxi ranks are shown on various town plans in the text (see italicised type in index for town maps). On pages 130-132 you'll find the current public transport timetables, but *please do not rely solely on the timetables in this book*; changes to scheduling are fairly frequent. Obtain a listing from the Tourist Office in Palma (Avenida Rey Jaime III) as soon as you arrive! Finally, do remember that local transport will be much busier on Sundays and holidays.

PALMA DE MALLORCA
principal streets
transport departure points
city exits for motorists

500m
0 ——————————— ¼mi
▲ N

← Pueblo
Español

← Bellver

A

Departure points

🚌   all depart from station, Plaza España
🚌a Bar Ca'n Meca, Archiduque L Salvador
🚌b Bar Curry, Archiduque L Salvador
🚌c Bar Rio, Archiduque L Salvador
🚌d station, Plaza España
🚌e 7 La Rambla (Via Roma)
🚌f Bar Kito, 4 Calle de Aragón
🚌g Bar Corona, 8 Calle de Aragón
🚌h Café Alcalá, Avenida A Rosello

Where to find your transport in Palma

Destination	🚌	Destination	🚌	Destination	🚌
Alaró (also 🚆)	d	Campanet	f	Pollensa and Port	d
Alcudia and Port	d	Ca'n Picafort	d	Porto Cristo	d
Andraitx and Port	e	Colonia San Jordi	h	Porto Petro	h
Artá	d	Deiá	a	Puerto de Soller	a
Banyalbufar	c	Esporles	c	San Telmo	e
Bunyola (also 🚆)	b	Estellenchs	c	Santa Eugenia	g
Caimari	h	Felanitx	d	Santa María	🚆
Cala Bona	d	Inca (also 🚆)	h	Santanyí	h
Cala d'Or	h	Manacor	d	Selva	h
Cala Ratjada	d	Moscari	h	Ses Salines	h
Cala San Vicente	d	Paguera	e	Soller	🚆
Calas de Mallorca	d	Petra	d	Valldemossa	a

Key

🚌 bus departure points (a–h)
🚕 principal taxi ranks
⛽ principal petrol stations
 1 museum (arts and crafts)
 2 town hall
 3 police station
 4 post office
 5 US consulate
 6 British consulate
 7 tourist information*
 8 Oleza palace
 9 Marques de Palmer palace

10 Arab baths
11 Episcopal palace (museum)
12 cathedral
13 military headquarters
14 Almudaina palace (museum)
15 La Lonja (fine arts museum)
16 maritime museum
17 Club Náutico
18 St Eulalia church
19 San Francisco church
20 market
21 hospital

also information kiosk in the Plaza España, opposite the station

☀ Picnicking

Picnicking can be great fun on Mallorca, provided you choose either an established picnic site created by ICONA or an open area along the course of one of the walks. Much of Mallorca's land is in private hands — although it might *appear* to be open countryside. So **never** cross boundary fences, or picnic in enclosed fields, or you might find yourselves confronted by an irate landowner!

ICONA

These letters stand for El Instituto Nacional para la Conservación de la Naturaleza. Our National Institute for Nature Conservation has recently taken over several areas of the island, to convert them into beauty spots for public enjoyment. ICONA has also created several picnic areas, which were sadly lacking on the island — three of these being on the C710 between Lluc and Pollensa. They're very well equipped, with special brick ovens for roasting meat, wooden trestles and benches under the trees, outdoor water taps and modern WC facilities. Everything is spread out, so that you're not 'on top of' everyone else!

Other ICONA areas include the picnic site near the Playa de Coll Baix on the Aucanada peninsula (Walk 22) and the extensive area of the Cairats valley, near Valldemossa (Walk 5).

All *roadside* picnic areas *with tables* (and sometimes other facilities) are indicated both in the car tour notes and on the colour map by the symbol ⨉.

Picnic suggestions

If you prefer a 'get away from it all' picnic — or if you find that the established sites are too crowded (possible in the summer season and on Sundays and holidays), why not try a picnic spot along the course of one of the walks?

All the information you need to get to these 'private' picnics is given on the following pages, where *picnic numbers correspond to walk numbers*, so that you can quickly find the general location on the island by looking at the colour map. Under each picnic description, you'll find walking times, map reference and transport details (🚌, 🚃 means that the picnic is especially suitable for those using public transport — either bus or train; 🚗 indicates a picnic spot most suitable for those travelling by car). The exact location of the picnic spot is shown on the appropriate *walking map* by the symbol *P*, printed in green.

Please remember that these picnic suggestions are 'off the beaten track': you will want to wear sensible shoes and perhaps a **sunhat** (○ alerts you to a picnic spot in full sun). It's a good idea to take along a plastic sheet as well, in case the ground is damp.

To help you choose an appealing picnic place, a photograph is included for each suggestion — showing either the setting itself, or the views to be had from the picnic spot.

If you're travelling to your picnic by public transport, refer to the timetables on pages 130–132. Here you may find more convenient scheduling than that given for the corresponding (long) walk. **If you are travelling in a hired car,** watch out for animals and children on the country roads, and always drive carefully through villages, where children often play in the streets. Without damaging plants, do park *well off* the road; **never** block a road or track!

All picnickers should read the country code on page 60 and go quietly in the countryside.

1 Vista Dragonera (map page 65, photograph page 65) 🚌 🚗

Choose shade or sun for this picnic, on a low headland overlooking the Isle of Dragonera. Only 15-20 minutes walking from the bus stop, or a couple of minutes on foot if you come by car.

Turn right at San Telmo, skirting the headland and following signs to 'Vista Dragonera'. Just before the tarmac road ends, turn up right on the earth track to park and picnic.

2 Esporles (map page 67, photograph page 66) 🚗

Five to ten minutes walking from your car takes you to good picnicking in sun or shade, with countryside views.

Follow the road signed 'Es Verger' from the centre of Esporles, and use the notes on page 67 to start Walk 2.

3 Alquería d'Avall (map page 68, photograph page 68) 🚂 🚌 🚗

Sunny or shaded picnicking overlooking olive-studded terraces, about 35 minutes' walk from the railway station. If you have a car, leave it at the Ca'n Penasso restaurant on the C711, saving a good 10 minutes.

Use the notes on page 68 to find the overlook, just past the second gate of the Alquería d'Avall farm.

4 Puig de Santa Eugenia (map page 70, photograph page 71) 🚌 🚗 ○

About 20 minutes' easy climbing up from Santa Eugenia leads to a sunny picnic spot overlooking Es Pla (the plain). Can be windy in winter!

Your objective is the cross monument above the town; it's hard to believe, but from here almost the entire island is visible! This picnic walk starts from the Plaza España, the main square in Santa Eugenia, an uphill climb from the main road (PM304). You can leave your car here. Pass the bank and continue up the steep, winding tarmac road. Once onto a level tarmac track, turn right, and then left at the end, to go up a stony, walled-in track. Go through the gap in the wall at the top end of this track, to find the narrow, overgrown footpath up to the top of the hill. Climb the low stone wall and continue up to the cross monument.

5 Valldemossa (map page 74, photograph page 73) 🚌 🚗

A picnic shaded by superb umbrella pines, overlooking Valldemossa. Under 20 minutes' walking from the village if you come by bus, or about 5 minutes if you travel by car.

If you're on foot, use the notes on page 72 to begin Walk 5; you'll reach the pines in under 20 minutes. If you're in a car, you can leave it in the new housing estate below the pines, but park neatly and do not obstruct any estate drives! The road into the estate is the first turning north off the Valldemossa—Palma road (PM111); from here follow the notes on page 72 to the start of the track to the pines.

6 Torre Picada (map reverse of touring map, photographs pages 76 and 27) 🚗

Picnic at the tower, overlooking the sea, or below it on a grassy slope.
Use the notes on page 76 to drive up the Carrer de Bélgica, out of Puerto de Sóller, as far as the gates to the Torre Picada track. Leave your car by the gates, well tucked in. From here it's a walk of about 20 minutes to the tower, but there are good picnicking spots along the way as well. It can be windy at the cliff edge by the tower in winter, but there are sheltered, sunny — or shaded — spots below. *Take care if you picnic by the cliff edge, overlooking the sea!*

7 Es Barranc (map reverse of touring map; photograph page 79) 🚗

There's good picnicking not very far up the (steep) path of Es Barranc, on grassy terraces, populated by olive groves, overlooking the Sóller valley.
The starting point is really Biniaraix, a short drive from Sóller. Leave your car well tucked in, and use the notes for Walk 7 to follow a short way up the footpath signed 'Camí

Best reached by: 🚌 bus, 🚗 car, 🚆 train, ⛴ boat; ○ — in full sun d'es Barranc'. If you come by train, consider taking a taxi from Sóller station to Biniaraix: you'll have only a short 10-15 minute climb up Es Barranc weighted down with your picnic, and you can stroll back downhill to Sóller afterwards (about 45 minutes).

8 From the Mirador de Ses Barques (map reverse of touring map, photographs pages 83 and 27) 🚌* 🅿

A picnic in a sheltered sun-trap, by olive-planted terraces.

Leave your transport at the Mirador de Ses Barques and follow the notes for Walk 8 for as long as you like. There's good picnicking only 5 minutes into the walk, but if you go as far as the Font de Bálitx (20min), you'll find some welcome shade on a hot summer's day.

9a La Calobra (map reverse of touring map, photo page 55) ⛴ 🅿 ○

You can picnic on the beach, in the sun (and in the company of day trippers), or you can venture up inside the gorge, where there are many good picnicking spots − but very little shade.

Leave your transport at La Calobra and explore inside the gorge as far as you like.

9b Escorca (map reverse of touring map, photo page 84) 🚌* 🅿

Picnic spots abound at Escorca − in full sun or shade.

Leave your transport at the Escorca restaurant on the C710 and use the notes for Walk 9 to start down the path behind the old church of Sant Pere. You'll find good picnicking in two minutes − or overlook the gorge in 15 minutes.

10 Puig Mayor (map reverse of touring map, photo page 87) 🅿

Several superb picnic spots on the northern slopes of Mallorca's highest mountain − in sun or shade.

The starting point is the K2.2 marker on the La Calobra road, so this picnic is not easily accessible by public transport. Leave your car in the (small) parking area, making certain that you do not block the road! Follow the notes for Walk 10 as far as you like; there's good picnicking as soon as you finish the initial 15-minute climb. Perhaps the best spot is in the shade of the oaks (35min).

11 Gorg Blau (map reverse of touring map, photo page 88) 🚌* 🅿

Not far into the course of Walk 11 − just an easy stroll from where you leave your car or bus − there's excellent picnicking way above the C710, overlooking the Gorg Blau. If you prefer a picnic just beside the water's edge, choose the Cuber reservoir, an area under the protection of ICONA.

Use notes page 88; ten minutes' walking gives good views, but after 30 minutes there's a splendid promontory in shade.

🚌* see **STOP PRESS**, page 136, for bus details

12 Puig de Massanella (map reverse of touring map, photograph page 99) 🚌 ▣

A shaded 'sitja', just five minutes up from the Massanella gates.
Leave your transport at the petrol station on the PM213 south of Lluc. Walk downhill 150m (yds) to the Massanella gates on the right. Follow the track, forking up right before the farm building, to find the shady *sitja* on your right, by a rock outcropping. There are no far-reaching views, just mossy banks and the shade of oaks. For sun and views, you'll have to climb on for another 15-20 minutes.

13 Lluc (map reverse of touring map, photo page 17) 🚌* ▣

A shady picnic under five minutes' walking from the monastery.
Leave your transport at Lluc and go to the monastery forecourt. A narrow tarmac lane leads northwest, between the bar-café left and the monastery right. In under five minutes you'll come to a rocky outcropping on the right, with shade and splendid views. Further down the valley are some of the oldest olive trees on Mallorca and fields steeped in wild flowers — but picnic near the roadside, not on farmland!

14 Binifaldó (map reverse of touring map, photo page 93) 🚌* ▣

Sun or shade, and many good picnicking spots are to be found on the road to the Binifaldó spring-water bottling plant.
This picnic is especially suitable if you are travelling by car and find that the established picnic sites are full. You can park at the monastery at Lluc. From there, leave the monastery by the main gates. About 100m/yds along the secondary road, find a wooden gate on the left. Turn in here, and take the path to the right, through the football pitch. You'll follow a picturesque track and soon come to the Lluc picnic area, with tables. When the track meets the C710, turn left and walk about 100m/yds more to the ICONA sign by the K17.4 marker. Turn up this Binifaldó road and continue as far as you like (about 30 minutes).

15 Oratorio de San Miguel (map page 103, photograph page 105) ▣

A picnic by an old chapel, easily reached by car and very near to the Cuevas de Campanet. Not very convenient by bus — but an easy hour's walk from Campanet.
The charming Oratorio de San Miguel lies on the old Pollensa road, just south of the entrance to the Campanet caves, on the opposite side of the road. It is shown on most touring maps. If you approach it from Campanet, follow the (tortuous) village signposting for the caves, which take you to the old Pollensa road.

🚌* see STOP PRESS, page 136, for bus details

16 Mortitx (map page 107, photograph page 106) 🚌* 🚗

Picnic in a 'wild-west' setting of wonderfully-formed rocks and gnarled trees — there's little shade.

The gates to Mortitx lie between the 10 and 11 km markers on the C710, about 20 minutes' driving west of Pollensa. There's only room for one or two cars to park here; if you're not in luck, try one of the ICONA sites or Picnic 13 or 14. Follow the course of Walk 16 for as long as you like, but you'll find good picnic spots within 20 minutes at most.

17 Ternelles (map page 112, photos pages 18, 109, 110) 🚌 🚗

The walk to this picnic is longer than any of the others — about one hour. But it's a very easy walk along a country lane, with so much to see along the way, that it's highly recommended.

Most current motoring maps show a motor road leading from Pollensa as far as the Castell del Rei. In fact, you cannot drive to Castell del Rei, but only as far as the gates to the Ternelles farm. But even driving to Ternelles is not recommended; the road is very narrow, with little room to turn the car round, and there is only room for one car to park by the Ternelles gates. Far better to start out on this picnic in Pollensa, using the notes for Walk 17. You can see the Roman bridge and have ample time to enjoy the lovely country road to Ternelles. **Important note:** The picnic area is only open to visitors on Mondays; see the notes at the beginning of Walk 17 (page 109).

18 Puig de María (map page 112, photograph page 114) 🚌 🚗

A shady or sunny picnic, overlooking Pollensa or Alcudia's bay.

By car you can drive part way up the Puig de María (the lane lies on the south side of the PM220, by the K51.9 marker). Leave your car where the road ends, and climb up the route of Walk 18 for under 10 minutes for splendid views of Pollensa, or for 20 minutes to overlook Alcudia. If you come by bus from Palma, ask to be put off at 'Puig de María', and add about five minutes to the above times. If you come by bus from Sóller (🚌*), use the map on page 111 to find the lane to the Puig de María.

19 Puig de S'Aguila (map page 112, photograph page 114) 🚌 🚗 ○

A picnic in full sun, overlooking the Formentor headlands.

The starting point is the Hotel Don Pedro in Cala San Vicente. From there, use the notes for Short walk 19 to find your picnic spot in about 10—20 minutes easy climbing — there are many fine overlooks from 'Eagle Mountain'.

Best reached by: 🚌 bus, 🚗 car; ○ — in full sun

20 Boquer Valley (map page 113, photograph page 116) 🚌 📷

A picnic under pines, overlooking the Boquer Valley, a setting of special interest to bird-watchers — so take binoculars along!

By bus use notes for Short Walk 20 — a 35-minute walk. By car, park at the Boquer gates, saving 15 minutes.

21 S'Atalaia de Albercutx (map page 113, photograph page 117) 📷 ○

A short climb up the track to the Albercutx watchtower affords splendid views of the Formentor headlands, but no shade at all.

Leave your car at the Mirador d'es Colomer and follow the start of Walk 21 until you find a setting that pleases.

22 Aucanada Peninsula (map page 119, photographs page 118) 📷

Two picnicking possibilities on the Aucanada peninsula, both with ample shade. If you want to go by taxi from Alcudia, see the hints on page 63, to ask the driver to take you to one of the picnic spots and return for you in time for the last bus.

The first picnic overlooks Pollensa's bay and is reached from the Ermita de la Victoria (see touring notes, page 33). Park here and follow Short walk 22 up towards Peña Roja for at least ten minutes for good views — the best views are reached after 20 minutes' climbing. The second choice is Mount Victoria Park: follow car tour notes on page 33, but turn right just in front of the Bodega del Sol bar. Leave your car inside the park gates and picnic anywhere; the outlook over Aucanada's lighthouse is 1.4km past the gates.

23 Betlem (map page 121, photographs page 121) 📷

Superb views of both the coast and the Artá range.

Use the car touring notes on page 37 to find Betlem, east of the Colonia de San Pedro. Then follow the indications in the notes and on the map for Walk 23 to enjoy this picnic, walking only for as long as you like.

24 Cala Matzocs (map page 124, photograph page 123) 📷

A shady picnic overlooking a lovely, sandy cove — about 15 minutes' walking from where you leave your car.

Use the notes in *italics* on page 37, to find the road to Cala Estreta. Park here and then follow the notes for Walk 24 to picnic in the trees just beyond Cala Matzocs . . . or continue uphill to the Torre de Aubarca (illustrated).

25 Cala Guya (map page 124, photograph page 42) 🚌 📷

You can find sun or shade at the lovely beach of Cala Guya, but in summer you're likely to find an overspill of tourists from Cala Ratjada keeping you company — so best to make this an 'out of season' picnic choice.

Use the notes for Walk 25 to drive or walk from Cala Ratjada to Cala Guya, where you can picnic on the beach or on the rocky finger of 'Es Guyó'.

◉ Touring

The ideal way to tour Mallorca is by car, of course. Most of the island's roads are in very good condition; many have been re-surfaced in recent years in an attempt to improve driving conditions. The mountainous west coast is the most popular side of the island, with spectacular scenery that you must not miss. The east coast has its own distinct flavour, and touring here is especially enjoyable in spring or summer months when you can take advantage of the idyllic beaches.

The wonderful valley below Lluc's monastery (Picnic 13)

Car hire

Remember that it's wise to shop around, because car hire prices vary quite a bit. As a generalisation, prices at the local firms are lower than those of international chains.

Be sure that you understand the terms of the hire agreement that you have signed and what the insurance covers. You will need a current driving licence, and *only* those people whose licence numbers and names have been written on the agreement will be covered by insurance to drive the car. *Do* check the car carefully for damage before you take it on the road. You will also be expected to pay a (cash) deposit against insurance and a full tank of petrol when you sign the agreement; you will be refunded to the value of any petrol in the car when you return it. (And note that many petrol stations are closed Sundays and holidays!)

Motoring laws

All road signs on Mallorca are international, except for the 'give way' sign, which reads *ceda el paso*. The motoring laws on the facing page are strictly enforced.

The Ternelles Valley in May (Car tour 4; Walk 17; Picnic 17)

Walk 1, which visits an ancient Trappist monastery, begins here in the island's western-most village. If you'd like to stretch your legs, why not try one of the short versions of this walk? You'll be passing the starting point when, after arriving in San Telmo, you turn right and continue along the coastal road until it comes to an end at 'Vista Dragonera', from where you have superb views of that island (and excellent picnicking just on the headland to your right — *P*1; photograph page 65).

Rejoining the C710 (53km), we wind up through a green landscape of pine-clad hills and mountains towards the rugged, western coastline of steep cliffs and rocky inlets.

A colourful fishing boat at Puerto de Andraitx (Car tour 1)

We begin to catch glimpses of the sea again now, and soon we can stop off at the Mirador de Ses Ortigues (63km ▣). Climb up the fallen rocks to the right for a good view of the rocky cove of La Cala de Ses Ortigues below. The coastal road continues now, affording excellent vistas all along, passing by a second viewpoint (65km ▣). Then a few more minutes brings us to the attractive cliff-top restaurant of Es Grau (67km ✕) and the adjoining **Mirador R Roca★** (▣). Take the stone steps at the right of the parking area up to the *mirador*, for some really splendid views of this wild and rocky stretch of coast.

The C710 now dives down through the tunnel of Es Grau and hugs the coast. At the Coll d'es Pí (71km ✕🅿▣), the road turns inland and down into **Estellenchs** (72km ♦♨✕). The village sits at the foot of Mount Galatzó, where orange groves and olive trees populate the fertile terraced slopes, irrigated by mountain springs. The road narrows as it leaves the village and snakes its way to the **Talaia de Ses Animes★** (78km ▣). Cross the narrow bridge to climb up inside the old watchtower (*talaia* in Mallorcan dialect) for more magnificent views of the coast. Futher along, we come to **Banyalbufar** (81km ♨✕), set on slopes above the sea. From here the road swings inland once more, as it winds through thick pine forests. Past some sharp bends, and just before the junction of the PM110, you'll find space to stop the car for a fabulous view of the mountains to the northeast around Valldemossa. Then fork right towards Esporles.

We pass a road off right to Puigpunyent and then find the signposted entrance to **La Granja★** (89km). This large and splendid house once belonged to Cistercian monks, and later to an aristocratic Mallorcan family, but the archways and ornamental fountains evoke its Moorish past.

On the homeward route, a lovely avenue of planes welcomes us into **Esporles** (92km ♦), a village built along both sides of a stream. You might like to visit the 13th-century church. The road in the centre of the village, signposted to Es Verger, is the starting point for Walk 2 and for a quiet countryside picnic (***P*2**; photograph page 66). Past Esporles, meet a junction at 93km (🅿) and take the right-hand PM104, coming to **Establiments**, where Chopin and George Sand lived before taking up residence at Valldemossa. The final stretch (🅿 at 101km) brings us to Palma at the joining of the Via Alemania and the Avenida Conde Sallent (104km).

Opposite: the green terraces of Banyalbufar in February. The secret of these well-kept, fertile plots is the irrigation system. Waters from mountain springs are channelled to them in canaletas (see page 127).

2 PRETTY MOUNTAIN VILLAGES

Valldemossa · Puerto de Valldemossa · La Ermita de la Trinidad · El Mirador de Ses Pitas · Son Marroig · Deiá · Lluc-Alcari · Puerto de Sóller · Gardens of Alfabia · Palma

86km/53mi; about 4 hours; Exit B from Palma (map page 9)

On route: ✗ at Ermita de la Trinidad; Picnics 3, 5, 6; Walks 3, 5, 6

This drive takes only a few hours, but I suggest you make a full day of it – there are so many interesting things to see and places to visit along the way! Entrance tickets are available at the gates for:

The Carthusian Monastery (Valldemossa): open daily except Sundays from 09.30–13.00 and from 15.00–18.30 (17.30 in winter); closed some holidays

Son Marroig (Deiá): open daily 09.00–12.00 and 15.00–20.00

Alfabia Gardens: open daily except Sundays from 09.30–13.00 and 15.00–18.00 (17.00 in winter); closed some holidays

From the Avenida Conde de Sallent, take the Calle 31 de Diciembre (Exit B — the beginning of the C711 to Sóller and signposted). On the outskirts of town, passing by the Red Cross clinic on the right, follow the signs that read 'Valldemossa', out onto the country road, the PM111 (✿ at 9km). At the junction (10km) keep right, following the sign to Valldemossa, through almond orchards and farmlands, towards the lower, pine-covered foothills below the *sierra*. The glass-blowing factory on the left, at **Esglaieta** (11km), makes a brief, but interesting stop-off. Now the road starts to climb gradually, through vast olive orchards and pines, towards the picturesque mountain village where Chopin and George Sand lived during the winter of 1838-9. The blue-topped bell-tower of the monastery where they rented cells is clearly visible from the road as it winds its way on up between the low hills.

Enter **Valldemossa★** (17km ✿✿✿✗P5): turn left, and then right, and you can park in front of the monastery. Originally the site of a Moorish palace, the buildings were later the retreat of King Sancho. After his death, the place was given to Carthusian monks who, little by little, constructed the monastery. When this religious order was expelled from Spain in 1835, private owners took over and rented the cells to travellers (the famous Spanish poet, Ruben Dario, also lived here for a short while at the beginning of this century). Join the throngs to visit Chopin's quarters, which contain his piano, death mask and some original manuscripts. The old pharmacy is fascinating. The church, of neo-classical type, is especially interesting because of the frescoes painted in the vaults by Miguel Bayeu, brother-in-law to Goya.

Leave the village along the main road, in the direction of Andraitx—Soller (signposted). At 19km, the C710 branches off right towards Deiá. But we'll continue ahead for another few hundred metres, and find a narrow turning off right. Drive *very carefully* down this narrow, tortuous road, which twists its way down the mountainside towards the sea, where the hamlet of **Puerto de Valldemossa** (23km ✕) shelters amongst the rocks. Quaint little fishermen's dwellings crowd around the tiny marina and straddle up the rocky hillside.

Return to the coastal C710 now, and turn left towards Deiá (★ at 28km). But just about another kilometre further along, keep a sharp lookout for the narrow turning up right to the **Ermita de la Trinidad** (29km ✦♠☎). The way is so narrow that only one car can get through — so hope that you don't meet anybody coming in the opposite direction! However, once at the top, there is plenty of room for parking and turning. Visit the tiny chapel and small interior patios, from where you can enjoy a truly marvellous view of the coastline below.

Again rejoining the C710, sitting on the clifftops almost opposite the turning up to the *ermita* is the **Mirador de Ses Pitas** (30km ✕☎). From this viewpoint, you can see the old house at S'Estaca, where the Archduke Luis Salvador spent many hours with his young lover, Catalina Homar. Continuing along the coastal road (✕ at 32km) and passing through Miramar (an early acquisition of Luis Salvador), we begin to catch glimpses of La Foradada (the rock pierced with a hole), a rocky promontory jutting out into the sea. It's not long before we come to **Son Marroig★** (34km ✕☎M), the principal residence of the archduke (see opposite).

Our route continues along the coast, passing by another viewpoint (☎) at 35km, and soon comes into the pretty mountain village of **Deiá** (37km ✦♠✕M), home of many well-known artists and poets — Robert Graves being one of the earliest to settle here. A stop-off can include a visit to the small but extremely interesting archaeological museum

Son Marroig: the rooms contain the original furniture, paintings, portraits and photographs of the family, and several of his sketches. Before you leave, see the marble mirador (at the left in the photograph). It was specially made for him in Italy and transported to Mallorca, where it remains a poetic reminder of a romantic past.

and the church on the hill above the village, which has a charming cemetery. A small road leads down to a pebble beach at the Cala de Deiá. The C710 twists its way through the village and then weaves between mountains and the rocky coast towards Sóller. On the way we pass through another artist's colony you might like to visit — the small hamlet of **Lluc-Alcari** (40km 🏔).

Continuing on towards Sóller (✕ at 43km), more splendid views unfold: the distant high peaks and lower mountains, pine-clad hillsides dotted with chalets, and later, the marvellous panorama of citrus and olive groves forming the basin of Sóller below in the valley. As you approach the village, turn left onto the C711 and head for **Puerto de Sóller** (50km 🏔✕). Here, amidst sun-seekers, bright bar-cafés and crowded beaches, the summer comes into its own. On the other hand, a rather desolate scene denotes the winter season. At any time of year, however, a short walk uphill to the Torre Picada (*P*6; photographs pages 27, 76) will be rewarded by a wonderful vista of the port and coastline.

Return along the C711 back past Sóller village (🍴 at 55km). Now the road begins to snake in interminable bends up towards the mountain pass, the Coll de Sóller. More superb views of the setting can be had from the *mirador* just below the pass (62km 📷). On the south side of the *coll*, we soon come to another viewpoint by a mountaintop restaurant (63km ✕📷), this time overlooking Palma bay.

Winding on down the mountain, through endless olive slopes, it is not long before we can again stretch our legs at the **Gardens of Alfabia★** (69km WC✕), while we explore the exotic pavilions, romantic arbours, and bamboo-shaded lily ponds. Our homeward stretch (✕ and *P*3 at 71km, 🍴 at 84km) brings us into Palma's *avenidas* at Exit B (86km).

3 THE MAGNIFICENT MOUNTAIN ROUTE

Sóller · Biniaraix · Fornalutx · Mirador de Ses Barques ·
Gorg Blau · La Calobra · Caimari · Selva · Inca · Palma

136km/85mi; about 6 hours driving; Exit B from Palma (map page 9)

On route: ✗ at the Mirador de Ses Barques and the PM213 between
Lluc and Caimari; Picnics 3, 7-12; Walks 3, 7-12

*This beautiful drive passes through some of the most spectacular
mountain scenery on the island, and it is generally the most popular
route. Therefore, although the roads are in good condition, heavy
traffic will slow you down considerably, especially in summer.
Expect to meet coaches. Many hairpin bends throughout, but
especially on the tortuous narrow road to La Calobra, make this a
route for the experienced driver only. Of all our tours, this is the
one you must not miss — so do consider a coach tour, if you want a
more relaxing day*

Leaving Palma from the *avenidas*, we take the C711 out
of the city (Exit B), in the direction of Sóller (♨ at 2.5
and 3km). You'll see the grand old country mansion of Son
Amar, now sadly converted into a tourist barbeque spot.
On a bright morning early in the year, this road is at its
best. It heads straight as an arrow across the plain through
dazzlingly bright pink and white almond orchards towards
the sombre mountain range beyond, where the sun has not
yet lighted the *sierra*. We pass by ✗ and *P*3 at 15km and
the **Gardens of Alfabia★** (Tour 2) at 17km. Then the road
starts to climb in earnest, winding up to the south side of
the Coll de Sóller (23km ✗⛾), with splendid overviews of
the plain and Palma's bay. Then, just over the pass, we find
a second *mirador* (⛾), from where the panoramic view of
Sóller in the valley, entirely surrounded by high mountains,
is breathtakingly beautiful. Go *carefully* now, round countless hairpin bends, watching out for tourist-loaded coaches
on the tight corners. At the first opportunity, we leave the
C711 at a signpost, turning right into **Sóller★** (33km ♨♨✗).
The village is a popular tourist destination not only because
of its setting, but it's also such fun to get about here, on the
charming narrow-gauge railway and the tram to Puerto de
Sóller. Drive slowly down the narrow streets (you may find
the sketch-map opposite helpful), to come to the Plaça de
Sa Constitució (Constitution Square). Before us is the 16th-
century church, with its lovely façade (see page 81).

Continue on round the square and you'll soon see the
signpost to Biniaraix — pointing us to the right, down a
narrow but animated street, full of busy shoppers, where
the tangy scents range from carved olive-wood to freshly-
baked bread. Driving — again, very slowly — along this
narrow road, we continue on to **Biniaraix** (35km ♨ and *P*7).
Many mountain footpaths radiate from this quaint little

village nestling in the mountains amongst orange groves; one of the best is the old pilgrims trail up Es Barranc (see footnote page 77 and photograph page 79). In the hamlet, turn right into the Calle San José, a very narrow street. At the end, turn left down an equally narrow lane that leaves charming Biniaraix behind, winding on between beautiful chalets and orange orchards. There are some excellent views of Sóller from here.

Coming now to a wider road, we turn right, passing by the stream, and come into **Fornalutx** (37km 🚻✗), which must surely be the most picturesque village on Mallorca. You can park in the small leafy square and explore up the stone steps, along quaint cobbled streets, where open doorways show beautiful Mallorcan interiors. And you'll probably want to visit the old church.

From the square at Fornalutx, take the continuing road to the right, which now climbs up above the village, through a scenic landscape of orange groves and olive orchards on terraced slopes. Here, also, there are some wonderful vistas of the Sóller Valley. Eventually we come to the road junction, where we turn right on the C710, in the direction of Lluc and Pollensa (signposted). This mountain road climbs to amazing heights, affording breathtaking views of the valley and coastline, before we come to the fabulous **Mirador de Ses Barques★** (40km ✗☞✗ *P*8),

The Mirador de ses Barques is famous for freshly-squeezed orange juice and fabulous views over Sóller's bay, with its port and lighthouse. The Torre Picada (Walk 6) on the headland can also be seen at the right. Before you leave the mirador, use the notes on page 81 to stroll towards Bálitx. In five minutes you'll come to the lovely stone-walled olive terraces shown on page 83 (Picnic 8).

Leaving the Mirador de Ses Barques, continue along the ever-climbing C710, passing more olive-terraced slopes and pines, heading towards the peaks. We can see the enormous Puig Mayor (1445m/4740ft) looming up ahead, and the air is decidedly fresher. After climbing steadily for a while, we come to a short tunnel (41km). Then, after passing a deep, terraced valley down below on the right, we meet the first long tunnel under the mountain (switch on your car lights), at the Coll d'es Puig Mayor (48km ☜).

Say 'goodbye' now to this scenery, or take your last snapshot from the viewpoint, for you will find that the landscape is completely different on the other side. Once your eyes have accustomed themselves to the daylight again, a tranquil, uninhabited panorama of green valleys and rocky mountains unfolds itself before you, as the road winds down to the Cúber valley, passing through the military zone of Son Torrellas. (Do not attempt to take photographs while driving through this area — your film might be confiscated.)

Soon we come to the Embalse de Cúber (☜), the Cúber Reservoir, starting point for Alternative walk 7. Past here, we cross a modern aqueduct (*P*11) and round the south side of the Puig Mayor over to our left. Then we arrive at the second — larger — reservoir, the **Gorg Blau**, built in 1971 (54km ☜; photograph page 88). Across the water, the keen eye can find some prehistoric columns, part of an ancient temple dating from the 5th century BC. Then we pass through a second tunnel and leave the valley.

It's not long before we reach the turn-off to La Calobra (PM214-1) at 56km. The narrow, but fairly well-surfaced road climbs over the bare mountain (*P*10 at the K2.2 marker; photograph page 87) and then finds its way to the sea. Many sharp bends later, we arrive at **La Calobra** (68km

Selva in February, surrounded by flowering almond trees. The hilltop village is dominated by its square-towered church. Folklore festivals are held here on Tuesdays and Fridays throughout the year

▲✕), a beautiful creek. Here, some of the most stunning and grandiose island scenery can be contemplated, at the **Torrente de Pareis★** (the twin streams), where a torrent flows between vertical rock cliffs almost 200m (535ft) high, towards the sea. A small shingle beach (*P*9a; see page 55) is reached through an exciting tunnel under the rock. Boat trips run daily throughout the summer (see schedules page 132), and, if the sea is calm, this is decidedly the best way to view this wonderful part of the Mallorcan coast.

Return now to the C710 and pass under a lovely russet-stone Romanesque bridge spanning the road (81km). Turn left in the direction of Lluc (signposted), following the mountain route. Soon we can stop for a few minutes at the tiny Mirador de Escorca (84km 📷), where, looking over the precipice, we can really appreciate the tremendous height of the gorge. Across the valley, the *carabineros'* large old house (Walk 13) can be seen, abandoned on the hillside. Just beyond the *mirador* we find the chapel of Sant Pere (85km ⓘ✕), on the left, opposite Escorca's restaurant. You may ask for the key at the restaurant: this is one of the oldest historical monuments on Mallorca. It's from this churchyard that the path (*P*9b; photograph page 84) leads down into the gorge of the Torrente de Pareis (Walk 9).

From Escorca we continue as far as the next road junction (90km), where we meet the turning left to Lluc. Today we continue straight ahead however, in the direction of Inca (signposted) on the PM213 (⛽ left), passing by the gates to the Puig de Massanella on the right (*P*12). We wind on down through the mountains, between pine- and oak-covered hills and valleys (📷 with parking on the right at the first S-bends, followed by ✕ on the left). Pass more olive-terracing and then come into the pretty village of **Caimari** (100km ⓘ), at the foot of the *sierra*. There's a lovely, easy walk from here to Binibona — see Short walk E, page 100.

Leaving the village we come upon undulating country-side, almond- and olive-covered foothills, and arrive shortly after at **Selva** (102km ⓘ), set on a hill (see photograph opposite). Our next centre is **Inca** (106km ▲ⓘ✕⛽⊕), famous for its leather factories and wine cellars. Shoemakers have congregated in Inca since the eighteenth century, and a good export trade still exists. Inca's one-way traffic system demands a keen eye for the signposts to Palma! We meet the C713 and turn right for the last lap of the tour (the route is described, in reverse, on page 30). Now a straight and easy run brings us into the city's *avenidas* on the Calle Aragón (Exit C), after an exhilarating 136km drive.

4 THE SIERRA AND THE CAPES

Santa María · Inca · Lluc · Pollensa · Puerto de Pollensa ·
Cabo de Formentor · Alcudia · Puerto de Alcudia · Mal Pas
Cuevas de Campanet · Palma

203km/126mi; about 7-8 hours driving; Exit C from Palma (map p9)

On route: X on the PM213 between Caimari and Lluc, two
ICONA picnic areas on the C710 between Lluc and Pollensa, S'Illot
(Mal Pas), Ermita de la Victoria; Picnics 12-22; Walks 12-22

*Take a couple of days over this tour, if you can. If you make it a
one-day tour, do start out early in the morning. The beauty of the
capes is certainly worth the long drive from Palma (on excellent
roads), and a visit to the dream-like caves at Campanet (open daily
from 10.30—18.45) adds a perfect final touch to the excursion.*

From the *avenidas*, take the Calle Aragón (the road to
Inca — Exit C from Palma; ♣ at 2km). This becomes the
C713 and passes the suburb of Pont d'Inca at about 4km.
The road continues straight ahead, out into the country,
and across the flat lands of the plain (♣ at 7km; ✕ at 8km).

The first village met is **Santa María** (14km ✕♣⊕♦ and M
of natural history). The blue-belfried church is worth a visit,
as are the wine cellars and the leather goods factory (this
latter has an entrance marked by the trunk of a centuries-
old olive tree). Continuing along the C713, we pass through
Consell (17.5km ✕⊕) and a glassblowing factory on the left
just outside the village. **Binissalem** (22km ♦✕ and olive-
wood factory) is famous for its wines. Its church, which
dates back to the fourteenth century, is an interesting blend
of Gothic and Baroque architecture. Not much further along
is the **Foro de Mallorca★** (25km ✕M), a castle-like structure
housing a wax museum. Perhaps you've time at least for an
early-morning coffee by the pool.

We soon reach **Inca** (28km ♦▲▲✕♣⊕). Several leather
factories here sell their goods at amazingly low prices
(compared with Palma), but you would need a complete
morning just to browse, so today press on! Do not turn left
here into the city centre, but keep on the C713 as far as
the third set of traffic lights; here turn right, following signs
to Llubi; then *immediately* turn up left at the tiny roundabout for Lluc (the route is well signposted through Inca).

Once out into the country again (♣ at 31km), you'll
find the PM213 starts to climb steadily up into the foothills
towards the *sierra*, passing through **Selva** (34km, Tour 3),
and later winding on through fields of almond and olive
trees to **Caimari** (36km ♦), a picturesque village sheltering
at the foot of the mountains. Here our climb up to Lluc
begins, through thickly pine- and oak-wooded hills and
mountains. We pass by the first, shady picnic area (✕) at

30

The delightful valley near Orient (Car tour 5)

39km. As we climb higher, we come to the famous 'Salto de la Bella Donna' at 42km (📷). This is not a fully-fledged *mirador*, but there's just room to leave your car on the gravel over at the left-hand side of the road. Legend has it that a pilgrim pushed his wife over the precipice here, while they were making a pilgrimage to Lluc on foot. When he later arrived at the sanctuary, he discovered his wife praying tranquilly before the image of the Virgin. The panorama from the 'Salto' is exceedingly wild and beautiful.

Continuing up to Lluc, we pass the gates to the Puig de Massanella (*P*12) on the left and continue along (🍴✖ at 44km) until we meet a junction. Turn right here onto the C710 (✖ at 45km). Meet a second junction and fork up left (△WC) into **Lluc** (46.5km 🚻✖M✖*P*13; photo page 17).

The monastery of Lluc is steeped in history and legend, originating during the eighth century, when a young shepherd was reported to have seen visions and strange lights in the sky, whereupon he discovered a carved image of the Virgin. Years later, this was deposited in the church of Sant Pere at Escorca (see *P*9b and Walk 9), only to disappear and re-appear once again at Lluc — where a small chapel was then built. The present monastery building dates from the seventeenth and eighteenth centuries; the church itself, built between 1622 and 1724, was considerably altered at the beginning of the 1900s. Visitors come from all over the island to this important Catholic centre, and pilgrimages are often made on foot up to the sanctuary. An interesting museum contains coin collections, typical dress, and items of archaeological merit. Of most importance to lovers of Mallorca's countryside is the opportunity to stay overnight at the monastery — for this is the very best spot on the island from which to start on several superb walks!

From Lluc follow the C710 towards Pollensa, past two ICONA picnic sites (**✗**WC) and some more secluded picnic spots (**P**14, 16, 17; photographs on pages 18, 93, 106, 109, 110). The narrow road snakes through a dramatic — almost savage — landscape of bare mountains (see photograph on page 108), towards the northern end of the island and a magnificent vista over Pollensa's bay (**✗** at 64km).

Come to **Pollensa** (66km **♦♦✗♟**), a market garden town. By the side of the road, near the entrance to the town, and almost opposite the signpost to Ternelles (**P**17), a Roman bridge **★** — the only one of its kind on Mallorca — still stands over the Torrente de San Jordi. Visit the cypress-bordered stone stairway that leads up Calvary Hill★ to a tiny 18th-century chapel, from where there is a glorious view of the bays of Pollensa and Alcudia. There are 365 steps, one for each day of the year. From here you can also see the Puig de María (333m/1090ft; **P**18; photograph page 114), almost opposite, on the other side of town. There's a sketch-map of Pollensa on page 111, which you may find helpful.

Leaving Pollensa, continue straight ahead (the route is now the PM220), to make for the port. You'll pass the side road off left to Cala San Vicente (**P**19; photo page 114) at 68km, and then come to **Puerto de Pollensa** (72km **♦♦✗♟⊕M**) — a touristic, but tranquil coastal resort looking out over the bay. Everyone will enjoy stretching their legs here, and the art lovers among us will surely pay a visit to the Anglada Camarasa museum of oil paintings and Chinese art, opposite the beach at the end of the promenade.

Just before you reached the sea front here at the port, you will have seen the (signposted) PM221 to Formentor branching off left. Return to this road and climb the bare rocky promontory (passing **P**20 at 74km). Several sharp bends later, arrive at the splendidly-engineered **Mirador d'es Colomer★** (78km 🎦). A walk along the footpath and up the steps leads to a precipitous viewpoint over the jagged rocks and sea, hundreds of feet below. The rocky Isla Colomer is best seen from here. Opposite the *mirador* steps, a tarmac path leads up to the old watchtower of Albercutx (**P**21), from where there are unsurpassed views of both Formentor and the Bay of Pollensa (photograph page 117).

Down over the other side of the pass now, the PM221 winds between sea and pines towards the magnificent Bay of Formentor, where pale turquoise and aquamarine waters kiss the white sands. Coming to a fork (81km), where a signpost to the **Cape of Formentor** points left, we can continue straight ahead to visit the famous Hotel Formentor.

Its opening in 1926 was heralded by illuminated advertisements on the Eiffel Tower; the 'jet set' and many famous film stars and other VIPs frequent this beautiful paradise by the sea. From here another eleven kilometres (along a fairly narrow and sometimes vertiginous road with two more *miradors*) bring us to the cape and its lighthouse, poised on the jagged cliffs — the home of Eleanora falcons.

Leaving the beauty of Formentor, we return to the port (116km), and from the seafront, continue ahead to Alcudia (signposted). This is another spectacular drive, following round the bay. At the junction signed Puerto de Alcudia or Palma, we turn left into **Alcudia** town (126km **i̇M✕**), once the Roman capital of Mallorca. Originally named 'Pollentia', this thriving Roman city flourished from the second century BC until the sixth century, when it was destroyed by invading Vandals. There are still some remains of the city walls, built during the reign of Jaime II, when the town bore the name of Alcudia, derived from the Moorish word for 'hill'. The museum contains items from Roman times.

Continuing on the C713, we come to traffic lights. Here we can turn right to the **Port of Alcudia** (129km **⚓✕**), famous for its freshly-caught lobsters, available in most of the sea-front restaurants. A long, wide beach stretches out into the distance, in front of hotels, sun-clubs and souvenir shops, and the wide marina reaches out into the sea, where ferries from France dock in the deep harbour.

On the way back to the town of Alcudia, be sure to visit the remains of the Roman amphitheatre, on your left, not far outside the town walls (signposted). After your visit, rather than try to turn round in this narrow lane, continue ahead to meet again the C713. Turn right to the traffic lights and then *immediately* left, onto the country road signposted 'Mal Pas' (*P*22). A short drive along this picturesque peninsula, through the splendid *urbanización* of Bon Aire (134km **✕**) and past the tiny islet of S'Illot (**✕**), brings us to the turning right to the Ermita de la Victoria (137km **i̇▲WC✕** *P*22). Both picnic settings are shown on page 118. ICONA also provides camping sites in this area, with modern facilities and places for lighting fires.

From the Ermita de la Victoria we go back to the traffic lights. Here the C713 offers a straight run of 52km back to Palma (ample **✕🍴**). But a final visit is a must: the 8km return detour to the **Cuevas de Campanet★** (*P*15; photo page 105) is well signposted. These fabulous underground halls are resplendent with dramatically lighted stalactites and stalagmites. The C713 leads us back to Exit C (203km).

5 THE DELIGHTFUL ORIENT VALLEY

Santa María · Alaró · Orient · Bunyola · Palma

58km/36mi; about 3 hours driving; Exit C from Palma (map page 9)

On route: no ✗; Picnic 3; Walk 3 (and the walk from the PM210 to the Castle of Alaró — brief account below)

A pleasant, short but scenic drive, through olive groves and sheltered valleys — suitable for morning or afternoon

Use the notes for Tour 4 as far as Santa María, where we take the first turning left just as the road widens out in the village centre. This is signposted 'Bunyola'. Pass by a square stone well in the centre of the road, and then take the first road right (PM202-1, signposted to Alaró). Once out on this quiet country road, you'll drive between almond and carob trees, through landscapes sprinkled with lovely chalets, towards the mountains. Soon the road bends to the right, after which we keep straight ahead, ignoring the various side-roads that lead off to *fincas*. Pass the tiny hamlet of Son Antem (18km), a small cluster of old stone houses. Now the road makes a turn to the left and begins to climb up gradually between the low, pine-covered foothills — an extremely pretty stretch of road — wending its way *tranquilamente* over the undulating landscape (📷 at 20km).

Soon we come into **Alaró** (21km 🛈), an agricultural and industrial village set at the foot of the *sierra*. There isn't a great deal to be seen here, although the old district of the village, where steep and narrow streets weave between the old stone houses, is very picturesque indeed. The PM202-1 curves into the village, passing by the big school on the left, and ends at the main through-road. Turn down right here, and keep straight on until you see the signpost to Orient. Turn right onto the narrow village street and at the crossroads keep straight on (along the PM210 signposted to Orient).

The narrow road passes between high stone walls, coming into the countryside once again. A great red-rock bluff on our left dominates the landscape (see page 97), and at 23km a sign indicates the start of the 7km (return) ascent to Alaró Castle atop the bluff (🔺). As the climb is about 600m/1965ft, allow about 4 hours for the return walk. The views of the great peaks to the north, setting off the Orient valley and the plain, are magnificent.

Hikers can spend the night at a hostel by the ruins of Alaró castle

34

The scenic car tour continues through olive orchards and right round the bluff (where you can see the small white chapel up at the top, next to the castle ruins). The road is in good condition, but very narrow in places — don't forget that you *will* meet other cars, though this is not a frequently-used route. Soon, L'Hermitage, a first-class country hotel suddenly comes up on the right (30km ♙✖) — a good place to 'get away from it all'. And not long after, we begin to see the fairytale village of Orient, set on a rise in the valley below.

Come into **Orient** (32km ♙♠✖), nestling at the foot of the Sierra de Alfabia. Park on the main through road, just outside the bar-restaurant, and explore up the old narrow stone steps that lead to the eighteenth-century church. From the church there is a magnificent panorama of pine-clad mountains surrounding the Orient valley, where quaint stone houses crowd together in narrow alleyways down the small hillside. Both of the restaurants in Orient serve the popular Mallorcan dish of *tordos con col*, roast thrushes in cooked cabbage leaves (only available in the winter season; see also page 127). If you're brave enough to try it, it's delicious!

From Orient we continue out of the village on the PM210, now in the direction of Bunyola. Take your time driving through this beautiful, unspoilt valley to enjoy the views of varied landscapes — open farmlands, high mountains and pine forests of unchanging splendour. The road winds up over a low, pine-wooded hill in a series of sharp bends, and then leads down again through the forest, coming gradually into more open country (photograph page 31).

Then we arrive at **Bunyola** (41km ♙⊕✖ *P*3), an ancient municipality dating from the time of Jaime I (the Conqueror). Drive on down through the village, keeping to the PM210, until you arrive at the small square and the signpost to Palma. Here you can park and visit the baroque church, as well as one of the many distilleries in the village, where anisette and the typical Mallorcan liqueur, *palo*, are made.

From Bunyola turn right (when coming in from Orient), following the signs to Palma, now along the PM201. Pass by the railway station and continue on for 1km until you meet the C711. By turning right here, and parking at the Ca'n Penasso Restaurant, you could explore a bit along the path of Walk 3 (see photograph on page 68), or even climb up to the *mirador* on Alquería Mountain. The main tour turns left on the C711 and makes for Palma. A straight run (♟ at 57km) takes us into the capital at Exit B (58km).

6 VILLAGES OFF THE BEATEN TRACK

Sineu · María de la Salut · Santa Margalida · Ca'n Picafort ·
La Colonia de San Pedro · Artá · Manacor · Petra · Sant
Joan · Algaida · Palma

192km/117mi; about 7 hours driving; Exit D from Palma (map p9)

On route: ✕ C712 at Ca'n Picafort; Picnics 4, 23; Walks 4, 23

*Although this tour can be completed in a day (not leaving much
time for stop-offs), it is ideally a two-day programme. Not all the
roads are in first-class condition. Market days are: Wednesday
mornings in Sineu (agricultural) and Tuesday afternoons in Ca'n
Picafort (touristic)*

Leave Palma from the *avenidas* along the Heroes de
Manacor (Exit D). Just after the junction, where the
ring road crosses, turn left on the PM301-1 in the direction
of Sineu (signposted). A fairly uncomplicated run through
the countryside, amongst almond orchards and low hills,
takes us past Santa Eugenia (*P*4; photograph page 71) at
18km. There are some sharp bends to negotiate at about
24km. Past the turning left to Sencelles, our route is re-
numbered PM314-1 (✖ at 28km).

Come into the agricultural village of **Sineu** (33km ⚊✕♟),
where we turn left at the 'stop' sign, following the main
street through the town. Here on Wednesday mornings a
lively open-air agricultural market fills the main square, a
tradition kept from as far back as the Middle Ages. People
visit from all over the island, and the ambience is one of
rural charm. In recent years, however, one or two stalls
have been set up to attract tourists, so you can now buy
delicate porcelains or copper pots between the vegetables
and the livestock. Following along the main thoroughfare,
keep left at each fork (♟ at 33.5 km — just down the turn-
off to Inca). At the end of the village, you will see a sign
to 'María'. Turn right here, and, at the end of this street,
turn *right* if you wish to visit the market, or else follow
left with us on the PM351 towards María.

This is a pleasant bucolic run over undulating countryside — quite different from the flat lands of the orchards
along the Inca road. Pass by a quarry at 36km and soon
come to the small country village of **María de la Salut**
(40km ⚊), completely hidden away from the whirlwinds
of tourism. These lands once belonged to the infamous
Ramón Zaforteza, whose cruelty earned him the name of
the 'Evil Count'. The local church has an interesting Baroque
belltower. On entering the village, we turn left, following
the signs to Santa Margalida. Then a second left, and,
finally a right, brings us to a crossroads at 43km. Here we
turn left onto the PM334.

36

Santa Margalida (46km ‡ — also called Santa Margarita) is set on a low rise and commands excellent views of the distant *sierra* and the plain. From here we follow the PM341 to Ca'n Picafort (signposted). The road bypasses Santa Margalida and heads for the coast, between plantations of fig trees, carobs, and almond orchards. Keep a sharp lookout for the turn-off right to Ca'n Picafort (52km).

Cross the main C712 (✗) and come into **Ca'n Picafort** (56km ♠✗⚑⊕), where a long wide beach stretches out into the distance, below the tiled esplanade.

Turn up any of the side streets and head back to the C712, where we make a left turn. The road cuts through shady pine forests and gradually comes out into more open countryside. Soon we pass a turn-off to Son Serra de la Marina, a small coastal urbanisation (68km) and, not long after, a pretty chapel with a belltower appears on the right-hand side of the road, opposite a grand old mansion.

The continuing C712 passes by the road to Petra on the right (at 70km) and starts to climb gradually through more pines (⚑ at 70.5km). We'll make a detour at 74km: turn left on the PM333-1 out to the **Colonia de San Pedro** (78km ♠✗). The colours of the sea here are unbelievable. There's a small beach in front of the bar-café on the seafront. Let's continue a little further on our detour, along this charming country road, so little visited by tourists. We pass by bright smallholdings and orchards, enclosed by honey-hued dry-stone walls — the rural scene set off all the better by the stark backdrop of the Artá range seen to the south. Soon we come to the *urbanización* of Betlem. Perhaps you'll make the time to leave your car at the end of the road and explore (**P**23; notes and photographs page 121).

Returning to the C712, again turn left and climb in a series of bends through the dramatic mountain landscape to **Artá** (96km ‡✗⚑M), once the private shooting grounds of Jaime II. There's so much to see in Artá, that one really needs to spend an entire afternoon here. To begin, let's take the northernmost road out of the village. This narrow country lane winds up desolate hills to the Ermita de Betlem (106km ‡), set high on the slopes. Up over the brow of the mountain, behind the hermitage buildings, a

For Cala Estreta (Tour 7, Walk/Picnic 24):
Leave Artá on the Cala Ratjada road (C715). Pass the road to Ses Paisses on the right after 300m. Then, 1km further on, turn left at the T-junction, pass the football ground, and then turn right. This is the Cala Estreta road; it is signposted 'Cala Torta'.

rocky trail leads to a viewpoint where a magnificent panorama of the wide Bay of Alcudia and the distant rocky
peninsula of Formentor unfold, with the Colonia of San
Pedro and Betlem below. Back in Artá town (115km) visit
the Almudaina, the site of a Moorish fortress, containing
the Sanctuary of San Salvador, where some remains of the
original wall still stand. The archaeological museum is also
worth visiting: one of the best on Mallorca, it contains
many important pieces, including five bronze statuettes
dating from the second century BC. Finally, you won't
want to miss the pre-historic site of **Ses Paisses★**, where you
can see the *talayots* (towers) of an ancient civilisation. The
site is signposted; the turn-off is shown on the map page 37.

From Ses Paisses, we continue on the C715 (**�** at 117km)
towards Palma, coming to **Sant Llorenç d'es Cardassar**
(128km ♦✗⊕). This ancient feudal village was donated by
Jaime I, in an attempt to re-populate the area after the Re-
conquest of Mallorca from the Moors in 1229. The road
then leads through open countryside to **Manacor** (136km,
Tour 7). Past Manacor, we turn off right at 140km, onto
the PM332. This narrow, pretty country lane brings us to
the lonely village of **Petra** (147km ♦♣M), birthplace of Fray
Junípero Serra, the Franciscan friar and missionary to the
colonies in North America. On entering the village, take the
first left, and then turn left twice more, to reach the small
house where he was born. To visit the house and its small
museum, ask for the key at No 15, further along the street.
If you wish to visit the Sanctuary of Bonany (♦♣), where
Fray Junípero preached his last sermon, return to the C715
(signposted for Palma), and you will find the lane to the
hermitage on your right. Near Petra, more *talayots* are to
be found at the picturesque hamlet of Ariany.

Our route leaves Petra on the PM322 and continues to
Sant Joan (154km), where one of the most popular *romerías*,
the 'Fiesta of Bread and Fishes', is celebrated just before
Easter, with special home-made pasties of fish and bread.

Instead of leaving by the road signposted to Palma,
continue through Sant Joan, and turn right, then left, to
follow the PM323 towards Sencelles (signposted). A little
further along, turn into the PM313-1, to head for Algaida
(signposted). By avoiding the C715 for a little longer, we
can appreciate the beautiful countryside of this area, not
often seen by tourists. The low hills and pine woods soon
give way to almond orchards dotted with figs. We rejoin the
main road at **Algaida** (169km ♦✗♣), from where it's a
straight run back to our setting-off point in Palma (192km).

7 THE PINE COAST AND THE ARTA CAVES

Manacor · Sant Llorenç · Son Servera · Cala Millor and Cala
Bona · Costa de los Pinos · Canyamel · Cuevas de Artá ·
Capdepera · Cala Ratjada · Cala Guya · Artá · Palma

195km/121mi; about 7 hours driving; Exit D from Palma (map p9)
On route: no X; Picnics 24, 25; Walks 24, 25
You'll need a complete day for this tour, as it's one of the longest.
All the roads are in good condition. Tickets for the Caves of Artá
purchased at the entrance. The caves are open daily (except Christ-
mas day) from 09.00–19.00 (17.00 in winter)

Exit D from Palma (Heroes de Manacor) becomes the
C715 and takes us directly to Manacor (♨ at 2km and
5km; many X), across flat open countryside dotted with
innumerable windmills. Pass **Algaida** (21km ♦X♨) and then
Montuiri (28km X⊕) in a landscape of low hills and pine
woods, cultivated lands and old farmhouses. The road
continues (♨ at 36km) into the village of **Vilafranca de
Bonany** (38km X) and then out into rolling countryside
again, until we reach **Manacor** (46km ♠X♨⊕♦M), the
second industrial town of Mallorca. This is the centre for
hand-carved furniture and the world-famous pearl factory,
Majorica★. Jaime II built himself a palace here, and you
can visit the Torre de Palau, one of the remaining towers
(at the back of the church in the Plaza del Rector Rubí).
This tower houses a small museum, containing prehistoric
objects of bronze and clay (found in cave dwellings in the
hills to the northeast of the town). There are also some
Roman remains, and Moorish ceramics. Manacor's church
is a combination of Gothic origin and neo-Gothic recon-
struction; here, the Municipal Archaeological Museum
contains remnants of mosaics from the paleo-Christian
basilica of Son Peretó near Artá, thought to be part of a
Roman town at the time of Plinius.

Following the road signs to Cala Ratjada, we continue
on the C715 (⊕ at 55km), coming into the agricultural
village of **Sant Llorenç** (55km ♦X), where we now take the
PM403 to the right. This pretty country lane winds over
low hills, between vegetable gardens and farmlands, into
Son Servera (62km ♦), an ancient municipality — one of the
first districts to be re-populated after the conquest of
Mallorca by Jaime I in 1229. Servera was the name of the
first feudal lord to receive these lands from the hands of
the conquering king. Its economy is now mainly based on
the cultivation of almonds, figs and carobs. We drive into
the village along the narrow street, coming to the square,
where we continue straight ahead.

A signpost to Porto Cristo, Cala Millor, Cala Bona and the Costa de los Pinos indicates a turn to the left, and at the 'give way' sign, we continue along the PM402-3 in the direction of Porto Cristo, coming out into the country again. At 64km, bear left towards Cala Millor (signposted) along the PM402-6 (✖ at 65km). When you come to the crossroads, keep straight ahead on the beautiful tree-lined avenue, soon arriving at **Cala Millor** (66km ♠ ✖⊕), a tourist resort where fine sandy beaches alternate with rocky coves, and hotels, bars and souvenir shops crowd together along the esplanade. Keep straight ahead for the beach, where you may park and explore, or get some refreshment at one of the beach-side cafés.

Or turn left with us, along the sea-front, following the coastal road, which quickly runs into **Cala Bona** (67km ♠✖), with its tiny, but very picturesque harbour. We can take any of the turnings up to the left now, to find the (signposted) road to the Costa de los Pinos (the Cape of Pines), where we turn right at the 'stop' sign. Driving along here (✖ at 68, 69, 70km), we pass by many beautiful homes, part of this new *urbanización* built amongst the pines. At 71km come to a road junction; turn right towards the 'Club de Golf', drawing nearer to the sea again (♠ ✖ at 71.5km). Keeping right along the Avenida del Pinar, the road starts to climb up towards the lovely **Costa de los Pinos** (74km ▣). From the viewpoint we can look down over the Pine Coast, and along to the beaches of Cala Millor and Cala Bona, sheltered by the distant headland that hides Porto Cristo from view.

From the cape we return to the crossroads past the golf club (77km) and take the PM403-2 on the right, signposted to Son Servera. Coming to the first road junction of several (80km), turn right for Capdepera and Artá along a narrower country road (✖ just past the junction). At the next crossroads, again turn right towards Artá (signposted), and, at the 'stop' sign, turn right yet again (✖ at 81km). At the following junction (82km) we keep straight on towards Capdepera, leaving the road to Artá on the left. We're now on the PM404, a very pretty country route that runs over low hills and through pine woods. We'll soon have to negotiate a series of tight bends over the last hill, where a large signpost welcomes us on behalf of the region of Capdepera. The road twists on down the opposite side of the hill, with some excellent views across the countryside.

Meeting a crossroads at 86km, we turn right on the PM404-2 towards Canyamel (signposted), passing by the

Torre de Canyamel (87km ✕), a square tower built during the fourteenth century over Arab and Roman foundations, and where the country people were able to take refuge during pirate sieges. Not long ago, this tower was converted into a museum, but unfortunately it is now closed, although the restaurant is still open. Continue on towards the coast, turning left at the roundabout (90km), towards the **Playa de Canyamel** (91km ♠ ✕). This is an exceptionally pretty bay with a fine sandy beach, protected on either side by high cliffs and bordered by pines — another 'get away from it all' place! Turning back to the roundabout, we double back on our tracks past the Tower of Canyamel, to take the turning on the right towards the Caves of Artá (signposted). Following along here on the PM404-2, we begin to climb above the beach at Canyamel and then find the entrance to **Las Cuevas de Artá★** (100km 📷).

A long stone stairway leads up into the enormous dark hole in the rock cliff. Tickets for the forty-five minute visit are purchased by the bar at the entrance; then we begin our fantastic journey into the caves, once the hideout of pirates.

We return to the PM404-2, heading in the direction of Artá, but at the next road junction (104km), we turn right towards Capdepera and Cala Ratjada (signposted). At the following crossroads we take the PM404 on the right to **Capdepera** (107km ♦ ✕), where a medieval fortress and walls

The medieval fortress and walls crowning Capdepera rise above a lime-green May landscape. Approaching the village on the PM404

Use the plan on the right to walk – or drive – from Cala Ratjada to Cala Guya, where you could picnic on the beach or on the tiny rock promontory seen in the foreground – Es Guyó (Picnic 25)

crown the top of the hill. You can visit the small oratory inside the walls, built by King Sancho during the fourteenth century, and a walk around the parapets gives a magnificent panorama of the bay at Cala Ratjada and the pine-wooded coast.

From Capdepera we continue along the main through road towards Cala Ratjada and Cala Guya. Taking the C715 towards the left, we soon come into the tourist resort of **Cala Ratjada** (110km ♙✕♟⊕). The picturesque little fishing port and the lighthouse merit a visit (keep straight ahead where the narrow road twists up the side of the cliff above the coast (111km 🖼)). The views from here are wonderful: endless sea and pines and rocky cliffs. Returning to the centre, turn right just before the church for **Cala Guya** (also called – and signposted – Cala Agulla); there's a sketch-map above. A short run between hotels and restaurants quicky leads to an idyllic, half-moon beach (114km), where we can explore over the sand dunes or make a short walk to Es Guyó or the Coll de Marina (*P*25).

Once again in Cala Ratjada, we follow the signs into the village centre and out into the countryside along the C715, towards Artá, bypassing Capdepera and the road to Cala Estreta (*P*24) up right at 125km.

There's not enough time today to visit **Artá** (127km ⚲✕♟M – see Tour 6) properly, but there may be time enough for a visit to the prehistoric village of **Ses Paisses★**, with its megalithic stone 'towers' (*talayots*). To get there, continue on the C715 towards Palma and, *at the first bend*, take the turning across to the left – just by a small thatched hut, crossing the railway line and then driving down the narrow lane for about 1km (129km).

Our excursion ends by following the outgoing route back to Palma, again past the countless windmills, now silhouetted against the setting sun. We come into the city by Exit D after 195km.

8 LAS CALAS DE MALLORCA

Campos · Felanitx · Cala Murada · Las Calas de Mallorca ·
Cuevas del Drach · Porto Cristo · S'Illot · Safari Park · Palma

171km/106mi; about 6 hours driving; Exit E from Palma (map p 9)

On route: no ✗; no picnics (but the Calas de Mallorca offer excellent
picnicking; no walks

*This excursion makes a full day's programme. Roads are good, but
you'll want to spend ample time at a few spectacular stop-offs!
Tickets are available at the gates for:*

*Caves of Drach (Porto Cristo): open 11.00–12.00 and 14.00–15.00
summer (Saturdays 12.00–14.00 only); open 12.00–14.00 winter*

Aquarium, Porto Cristo: open 09.30–19.00 daily

Hams Caves (not included in our tour): open 10.00–17.00 daily

AutoSafari Park of Son Servera: open 09.00–19.00 daily

L as Calas de Mallorca, or The Mallorcan Coves, consist of
a series of tiny bays and inlets, some with sandy beaches,
just below Porto Cristo. The coves are strung out along a
picturesque stretch of wild and rocky coastline. Later in the
day, our tour takes in two other tourist attractions: the
beautiful Caves of Drach, where you'll take a silent boat
ride across an underground lake, and an unforgettable safari
through an African animal reserve.

We take the motorway (Exit E from Palma), in the direction of Santanyí, turning left onto the C717 at 8.5km. The
route cuts through pines and almond orchards (🍴 at 11km,
✗ at 15km) and comes directly into the market town of
Lluchmayor (23km ✗🍴; see Tour 10). We then cross rolling
countryside (🍴 at 26km) before reaching **Campos** (36km ✗🍴;
see Tour 10). In Campos, we leave the C717, turning left
onto the PM512 to Felanitx (signposted). Crossing open
countryside and cultivated farmlands, we arrive at the large
town of **Felanitx** (47km 🏛✗🍴⊕ⓣ), a wine-making centre,
also noted for its thriving ceramics industry. The church is
built in the same honey-coloured stone as Palma's cathedral.

Cala Figuera (Car tour 9)

Capocorp Vey
Car tour 10

In the centre, we cut across town by the rather complicated one-way traffic system, down narrow streets, keeping a *very* sharp lookout for the signpost to 'Porto Colom' at the exit from Felanitx. We now travel on the countryside PM401, going round a small roundabout and continuing straight on, passing by a side road on the right which leads to the Sanctuary of San Salvador (Tour 9).

Carrying on through a landscape of low, pine-covered hills, we must begin to look for the road (PM401-4) to Cala Murada (signposted), which turns off to the left just by the side of a country restaurant (57km ✕). Follow this road for 2km, and then turn right (59km), through pine woods, into **Cala Murada** (62km ♠ ✕). Driving as far as the sea front, we discover a pleasant — not too large — sandy beach, just below the rocky headland; this popular beach is often crowded, especially at the height of the season.

Returning to the PM401-4, we now turn right, passing side roads leading down to small coves and tourist apartments. The road to Cala Domingos comes up next on our right (66km), in case you'd like to visit. The country road rambles on (✕ at 67km) over the low hills, mostly covered in scrubs and sparsely populated by pines. A series of bends leads us to the turn-off to the Coves of Mallorca (69km). Turn right and first pass a rather desolate-looking area, with a scattering of new hotels sitting ostentatiously on the rocks and looking terribly out of place. Here a multitude of stony tracks criss-cross down to the various coves of the **Calas de Mallorca** (73km ♠ ✕). The small rocky bays are certainly picturesque and provide very good picnic spots. Park your car and walk over the headlands, discovering the different *calas*, where small beaches hide amongst the rocks along this wild part of the Mallorcan shore. Paths lead from one cove to another, and the colours of the sea vary from the palest turquoise to deep blues and greens.

Returning to the main route (PM401-4), we again turn right; now the pine-clad hills are interspersed with almond orchards along this stretch. Soon a turning to the right (84km) takes us to the pretty cove of Cala Romántica

(85km ✕), another smallish inlet with a beautiful sandy beach in romantic surroundings, as its name implies. Again turn right, after rejoining the main northeasterly route, still making for Porto Cristo.

At 93km, just outside Porto Cristo, we turn right into the road to the fabulous **Cuevas del Drach★**. The Archduke Luis Salvador (see also pages 25 and 79) commissioned the French geologist, Martel, to explore and map out these wonderful caves, which the Archduke had discovered on his very extensive travels all over the island. Our visit will take about one hour: the guided tour goes through a labyrinth of stone passageways, steps and caverns — brilliantly and cleverly illuminated.

Returning again to the main route, almost at once we are in the coastal resort of **Porto Cristo** (95km 🏨 ✕), an ancient fishing port for many centuries. It is thought that this was also an important seaport during Roman times. The excellent aquarium overlooking the harbour is worth a visit, as are the Hams Caves, if you can afford the time.

Continuing straight ahead through the town centre, we follow the signs to Son Servera, turning right just in front of the memorial cross (Porto Cristo was the only Mallorcan village to suffer badly in the Civil War). The PM402-3 to Son Servera soon brings us to the turning off right to **S'Illot** (97km 🏨✕), a beautiful holiday resort boasting a wide and sandy beach. Carry on through S'Illot and then take the road opposite Cala Moreya up left to rejoin the main route (102km ✕).

It's now just over a kilometre to the turning right for the **AutoSafari Park of Son Servera★** (105km). A slow drive along the arrowed route through this African animal reserve gives good views of rhinos, elephants, giraffes, zebras . . . in their natural surroundings.

From the 'Reserva Africana' we return to Porto Cristo, where we keep to the right, in front of the memorial cross, in the direction of Manacor. At the end of the road, we turn right again at the 'stop' sign (112km), along the PM402 (🍴 at 113km, ✕ at 120km). This road passes the entrance to the Hams Caves. In **Manacor** (123km ✕🍴; description Tour 7) we turn left and then right, towards the square, following the signs to Palma. Finally, coming out into the C715, a straight run brings us back to Palma's *avenidas* at Exit D, after 171km.

Farmlands near Ses Covetes in early summer (Car tour 10)

9 SAN SALVADOR AND THE EAST COAST

Santanyí · Cala Figuera · Porto Petro · Cala d'Or · Porto
Colom · Santuario de San Salvador · Felanitx · Castell de
Santueri · Porreres · Palma

188km/117mi; about 7 hours driving; Exit E from Palma (map p9)

On route: ✗ at San Salvador; no picnics (but the *calas* offer some
splendid picnic spots); no walks

*The best time of year for this tour is spring and early summer; it fits
well into a leisurely one-day programme, with ample time for stops*

Vastly different from the mountainous regions of the
western coastline, Mallorca's eastern coast consists of
a series of small coves, where tourist resorts have sprung up
in recent years, burgeoning side-by-side with extensive
agricultural centres.

Leave Palma on the motorway (Exit E), using the notes
on page 43 (Tour 8) as far as Campos. But today there's
time to make a brief stop-off on the outskirts of Lluchmayor, at the 'Molí d'En Gaspar', an old windmill converted
into a museum. You'll pass it on the C717, just outside the
town.

From **Campos** (36km ✗🛱; see Tour 10), we continue on
the C717 through open countryside (🛱 at 38.5km) and soon
come into the village of **Santanyí** (50.5km ✗🛱⊕🛉), set in
some five kilometres from the east coast. Do not leave the
C717 yet, but keep on ahead, entering the ancient fortified
town, dominated by its church. From the village, *carefully*
follow the signposts to Cala Figuera, to join the PM610-2.

This country road comes out of Santanyí and into an
open landscape, passing a smaller side road off to Cala
Santanyí on the right. The road is wide here, and soon the
tang of fresh sea breezes announces our arrival at one
of the prettiest coves in Mallorca, **Cala Figuera** (56km 🏨✗),
scene of many an onslaught by pirates and Saracens in past
centuries (sketch on page 43).

To continue our route to Porto Petro, we must first go
back to Santanyí, where we follow the signs towards
Cala d'Or through the village. We rejoin the C717 for a
short time, passing a small side road up left (at 66km) that
leads up to the Sanctuary of the Consolation, a small
oratory built during the 17th century. Not long after, we
come into the hamlet of **Alquería Blanca** (68km 🛉). Continue ahead, taking a left at the next signposting towards
Cala d'Or, but keep a sharp lookout for the road to Porto
Petro which soon comes up on the right. Turn right on this
(signposted) road (✗ at 70km) and come into **Porto Petro**
(73km 🛉🏨✗), a small fishing village reminiscent of Porto

Cristo (Tour 8). You can sit here by the still waters of the harbour, under the colourful awnings of the bar-cafés, and watch the world go by for a little while.

From Porto Petro we can go directly to Cala d'Or: good signposting indicates the short coastal route. First we come into the tiny harbour of Cala Llonga, part of **Cala d'Or** (77km 🏖 ✗). You'll need time to explore this 'Golden Cove'. There's a truly beautiful beach, where the sea is an unbelievable shade of palest turquoise — patched with royal blue, and rocky inlets of aquamarine waters bite into the coast.

Find the road to Palma coming out of Cala d'Or, and follow the signs to Cala Ferrera next, coming to a roundabout, from where we continue along the Avenida Cala Ferrera. Cala Ferrera (80km 🏖✗), Cala Serena (81km 🏖✗) and Cala Esmeralda are smaller — but equally beautiful — coves adjoining Cala d'Or; visit them if you have time.

From Cala Serena we head for Porto Colom (signposted) on a narrow country lane across open farmlands dotted with almond orchards and bordered by dry-stone walls. Meet the PM401-2 at S'Horta, and here turn right for Porto Colom. A couple of kilometres along, turn right for the port, through a landscape of pines and low scrubs, sprinkled with villas. Come into **Porto Colom** (93km 🏖 ✗), a centuries-old important commercial port, now also a beautiful residential area and summer resort. Visit the lighthouse, following the signs to 'Es Tancat de Sa Torre', from where you will capture some excellent views of the coast, or find the pretty little cove of Cala Marsal, hiding between the cliffs.

Leaving Porto Colom, we make for Felanitx on the PM401 (✗🛢 at 104km). Pine woods and almond orchards cover low hills, and the mountain of San Salvador can be seen ahead on the left. At 113km, turn into the smaller road on the left, the PM404-1, where you will see the signpost to the Sanctuary of San Salvador. The road soon starts to climb the mountainside, winding through thick pine woods to the hermitage.

Many sharp bends later, we arrive at the **Santuario de San Salvador** (116km 🛏🏖✗ ✗🗺) at a height of 510m/1675ft. An impressive monument to Jesus Christ dominates the hilltop. In the 17th century, this hermitage also served as an *atalaya* (see page 126), communicating with the other watchtowers at Porto Colom, Montesión and Santanyí. On clear days, much of the eastern coast is visible, with the mountains of Artá floating on the clouds to the north, and the distant *sierra* closing the western horizon. The monks still run a hostelry here (see page 59). The chapel holds a 13th-century Madonna statue and a Gothic altarpiece.

Leaving the sanctuary, we return by the hairpin bends to the main road, turning left on the PM401, and coming into **Felanitx** (122km ✕♨, see Tour 8). Enter the town and keep straight ahead, passing by the municipal park along the Calle Bellpuig and coming to the square. Continue ahead, to turn left later along the Calle Major, looking for the signposts to Palma. Come to a second square, decorated by elegant palms, where we continue ahead. Then we see the signposts to Santanyí, along the Calle Santueri (C714). Follow this route now, to visit the remains of the thirteenth-century castle of Santueri.

A small side road leads off left at 126km, signed '**Castell de Santueri**'. The narrow tarmac lane winds through almond and fruit orchards, orange groves and vineyards (✕ at 129km), and then curves up to the castle (131km). (In the winter, stop at the large house on the second bend to ask for the key.) This castle was reconstructed over the remains of an ancient Arab stronghold during the thirteenth century. It is said that a Mussulman held out for eighteen months here, after the invasion of Mallorca by Jaime I, and it is easy to see how this could be possible! Built in a very strategic position, the stronghold rested on the top of a isolated mountain with steep drops on all sides.

Now we return to Felanitx (137km), from where we follow the signs to Porreres and Palma. Enter the town as far as the first 'stop' sign, to find the Porreres/Palma signs. We join the PM510, and passing by the stone cross monument, head into the countryside towards Porreres. The road traverses many vineyards and flat cultivated lands.

Come into **Porreres** (151km ♦♨). From here, you may wish to make a seven kilometre detour to the Sanctuary of Montesión (♦♦✕▣). If so, follow the signs for Lluchmayor, which bring you to the PM502 leading southwest out of the village. The road to the sanctuary is met on the left, almost at once. Like other island hermitages, it is beautifully sited, commanding ideal views, and provides food and lodging in simple surroundings (see also pages 59 and 128).

Our itinerary, however, now makes for Palma. The route is well signed in Porreres, and we join the PM503, passing the petrol station and making for open countryside. At the crossroads, in front of the 'Ermita de la Cruz' (153km ♦), turn right in the direction of Montuiri. At the 'stop' sign (C715) turn left to return to Exit D at Palma (188km).

10 THE SOUTH AND THE PUIG DE RANDA

El Arenal · Cala Blava · Cabo Blanco · Capocorp Vey ·
S'Estanyol · Ses Covetes · Es Trenc · La Colonia de San
Jordi · Campos · Lluchmayor · Puig de Randa and Santuario
de Cura · Palma

147km/91mi; about 6 hours driving; Exit E from Palma (map p 9)

On route: ✗ at Cura; no picnics (except at the coves) or walks

*Another all-day tour, ideally for summer, since it includes some of
the island's most beautiful and unspoilt beaches. We end up at the
Puig de Randa, from where the whole of this itinerary is captured in
one magnificent view of the southeast coastline*

Driving right down to the eastern end of Palma's
avenidas, keep left for the turning onto the motorway
(Exit E), signposted for the airport and Santanyí. Continue
along, past the airport turnoff, as far as the sign for 'Playa
de Palma', where we leave the motorway for **Ca'n Pastilla**
(7.5km ▲✗⬮⊕). This is the beginning of the extensive
sandy beach and tourist area of **El Arenal** (▲✗⊕). At the
traffic lights (⬮ to the right), keep straight ahead, as far as
the sea-front, and follow this alongside the promenade,
where an endless chain of hotels, bar-cafés and swimming
pools borders the left-hand side of the road. Countless
traffic lights and numbered *balnearios* are our constant
companions along here. When we reach the other end of the
bay, we turn to the left (by the sign to 'Cabo Blanco'), up a
steep hill bordered by souvenir shops and yet more hotels.
A road junction is met at the top. Here, at the 'give way'
sign, take the second turning on the right, in the direction
of Cala Blava (signposted). The PM601-4 finally takes us to
the end of this conglomeration of hotels, restaurants and
night-clubs, and escapes into the countryside between low
pines and scrub.

But it's not long before we reach the urbanisation of
Cala Blava (15km ▲✗) on the right, where modern villas
and low blocks of holiday apartments fringe the small
beach. This is our last view of the sea for some kilometres;
from now on cliffside roads carry us to S'Estanyol. The
PM601-4 continues towards Cabo Blanco, soon passing a
turn-off to another recent housing development, **Las
Palmeras** (17km ▲✗), on the left. The road from here
crosses a rather desolate landscape of rough terrain and
low scrub, where neither agriculture nor the frenetic pace of
tourism have yet disturbed nature (save for ▲✗ at 19.5km).
A third urbanisation, Bahía Azul, comes up like an oasis in
the desert at 22km (✗), after which the sporadic presence
of some pines begins to add more colour to the landscape.

Soon the road nears the coast again, running alongside the high cliff-tops on the right, and it will not be long before we're at **Cabo Blanco** (31km 📷). From this 'white cape', there are excellent views of a wild, desolate part of Mallorca's coast. Then the road swings inland, passing by the military quarters, and heads once more for open country. Pass by the turn-off to Cala Pí (🛖✖), a small resort set in a creek, and almost at once come to one of the most important prehistoric sites in the Balearics, at **Capocorp Vey★** (36.5km; sketch page 44).

The gates to the site are padlocked, but ask for the keys at the old farmhouse across the road, where the custodian lives. You'll also be given an explanatory pamphlet. Excavations carried out here have uncovered many important pieces, such as pottery, bone implements and grindstones, supporting the theory that prehistoric peoples lived in this settlement from about 3000 years ago up until Roman times. Unfortunately, the 'finds' have been taken to the Archaeological Museum in Barcelona. But a scramble over the megalithic blocks permits examination of the many chambers, where silence floods through the dry-stone doorways, evoking scenes of a bronze-age community, grinding their wheat and tending their fires.

Back on the move, we continue in the direction of S'Estanyol (✖ at 37.5km), bypassing the road right to Vallgornera and turning right on the PM601-5. Enter the not very exciting resort of **S'Estanyol** (48km ✖) and keep on down to the sea front. Here turn left for La Rapita, a small seaside place further along the coast, where many Mallorcan families (mostly from the Lluchmayor region) spend their summer holidays. The main road through **La Rapita** (✖ at 52km) leads away from the sea, but we take a side road off right at 53km, signposted 'Ses Covetes'. This narrow country lane meanders between old stone farmhouses where prickly-pear cacti ramble at random, for about another kilometre; then we turn right once more, driving through pines to the coast.

Come to **Ses Covetes** (56km ✖; photograph page 45) and turn right along the sandy 'road' at the end. Here, a stretch of white sand and clear blue waters extends into the far distance, and, just by the small rocky headland, a beachside kiosk offers good, cheap meals (in summer). We can also explore from here the fabulous, long white beach of **Es Trenc** (signposted). Turning back in the car, it's a short drive over the unsurfaced track between sand dunes to this lovely beach. It's surely one of the most beautiful on Mallorca — kilometres of unspoilt sand and sea, edged by dunes, and as yet untouched by tourism. Here there's some peace and respite from the usual touristic scene of the island's more popular resorts. Further along Es Trenc, nudists bathe in the natural surroundings of this paradisial beach, seen in the photograph below.

Head back to the asphalted road and turn right. At the junction one kilometre further on, keep straight ahead, through open farmlands, until you reach the 'stop' sign (✕), and there turn right. At the next crossroads, turn right again, back onto the PM601-4 (63km), which takes us through more cultivated lands. Along here, we come to various crossroads: at the first (66km), keep straight ahead, in the direction of Ses Salines (signposted), and at the second (68.5km), turn right onto the PM604, towards the Colonia de San Jordi (signposted). Some pine trees now break the monotony of the flat landscape (♠ at 70km).

To the right we see the salt pans and great white 'mountains' of salt. This is a rich and important ecological centre of the island, where ornithologists are in their element and can observe a variety of aquatic and migratory birds — including herons, sandpipers, ospreys, the rarer flamingoes, and sometimes even kingfishers.

At the next road junction, turn right once again to come into the **Colonia de San Jordi** (74km ♠ ✕♣). Take the left-hand fork, on reaching the petrol station, towards the picturesque port and the small pine-shaded beach, accessible only on foot.

Leaving the colony behind, we turn back up the main road (right from the petrol station), to follow the PM610 briefly. But turning left at the second road junction, following signs to Campos, we continue along the PM604 (✕ at 82km), until we reach the C717. Here turn left and into **Campos** (91km ♠✕♣).

The dramatic beauty of Es Trenc on a stormy winter's day

Fields along the C717, south of Lluchmayor. The plains of Mallorca are wonderfully varied and colourfully planted throughout the year

Designated *villa* as early as 1300, no less than five watchtowers were built in Campos in the fourteenth century. Drive straight into the village, passing to the left of the petrol station, and continuing along the main thoroughfare, where you'll come to the church. Should you wish to visit it (key available in the neighbouring house), art lovers will be able to admire a painting by Murillo, which originally hung in the Sant Blai hermitage not far from the village. Apart from this, Campos is basically an agricultural village and does not have a great deal to offer the passing tourist. Leaving Campos on the C717, continue on in a westerly direction through orchards and cultivation.

Soon we come into **Lluchmayor** (104km ✕🛏🚹M). The eighteenth-century church and the seventeenth-century Convent of Buenaventura are the main architectural highlights, while on the outskirts of the village (on the C717 to Palma) a stone cross indicates the site of a confrontation between the troops of Jaime III and the army of Pedro IV of Aragón. You might also take this opportunity to visit the small museum in an old windmill called 'Es Molí d'en Gaspar', on the C717 just *before* you enter Lluchmayor.

Today's tour leaves the centre of Lluchmayor on the PM501, where we follow the signs to Algaida. This is a picturesque country road that leads through pine-wooded hills and orchards. Soon the road to Randa comes up on the right (at 109km). Drive into the small hamlet set at the foot of the Puig de Randa, an isolated massif standing out from the central plain.

In **Randa** (109.5km ♦✗), driving slowly along the narrow street, find the signpost for the 'Santuario de Cura', following round to the left and then sharply up right on the PM501-8. The road starts to tackle the mountainside in a series of tight bends, climbing up through pines. Not very far along are the wide gates to the Santuario de Gracia (111km ♦⌨), founded in the Middle Ages, and once a hostelry. Set under the brow of an enormous scarp, the spot is certainly worth a visit, if just to admire the beautiful tiling in the small chapel. The views are already splendid just this far up the road, but we keep climbing, passing by another small oratory on the right — this one dedicated to San Honorato.

Finally, at a height of 548m/1800ft, we arrive at the **Santuario de Cura** (115km ♦▲M✗⌨). Leave the car in the ample parking area outside the sanctuary walls and enter a wide courtyard. Visits to the library and small chapel are a must. The ancient library contains many manuscripts, prayer books and other relics from the days of the thirteenth-century scholar, Ramon Llull, who was born shortly after Jaime I conquered Mallorca.

Apart from the historical value of the visit, there are glorious views in all directions from atop this *puig*: the southern coastline is clearly visible all the way to Palma, reaching down to Cabo Blanco and along to the Cape of Salinas, where a millpond-like Mediterranean caresses the shore. The island of Ibiza floats magically on a blue horizon on clear days, and the rocky offshore isle of Cabrera can also be seen. The long chain of the Sierra de Tramuntana rides on the opposite horizon, to the north, and the wide central plain stretches out below, dotted with countless towns and hamlets. On a clear day, Alcudia's bay is visible from here as well. A hostelry has been run at Cura for many years; anyone can spend the night (see also 'Where to stay', page 59 and 'Ermitas', page 128). Cura is also a very popular place for wedding receptions.

We wind back down the mountain, and from Randa, we turn right for Algaida on the PM501. Coming into the large village of **Algaida** (125km ♦✗), keep left, following the signs to Palma. Joining the C715 at 127km, we head left for the capital. After a tour of 147km, we come into Palma via Exit D, the Heroes de Manacor.

☀ Walking

This book covers about 250km — 150 miles — of some of the best walking on Mallorca. I can't claim that *all* the best walks have been included; some classic climbs in the northeast — for instance Mount Galatzó — have been omitted in favour of spanning a wider territory. I hope in this way to give walkers a better feeling for the great variety of island landscapes — pastoral byways, as well as dramatic panoramas.

I hope you'll also use this book, together with the bus, train and boat timetables on pages 130-132 to make up your own walk combinations: I've indicated where routes link up on the walking maps, and the large colour map shows the general location of all the walks. One word of caution: **Never try to get from one walk to another on uncharted terrain!** Only link up walks by following paths described in these notes or by using roads or tracks: don't try to cross rough country (which might prove dangerous) or private land (where you may not have right of way).

There are walks in the book for everyone:

Beginners: Start on the walks graded 'easy', and be sure to check all the short and alternative walks — some are easy versions of the long walks for experts.

Experienced walkers: If you are used to rough terrain and have a head for heights, you should be able to tackle all the walks in the book (except those labelled ⓖ) — taking into account, of course, the weather conditions and their consequences. For example, if it has been raining recently, some of the mountain walks will be unsuitable. Also, storm damage can make the way unsafe at any time. Remember, too, always to follow the route as described in this book. If you have not reached one of the landmarks after a reasonable time, you must go back to the last 'sure' point and start again.

Experts: You should not need a guide for any of the walks, provided you are used to sheer, unprotected drops and always use extreme caution.

G uides, waymarking, maps
Some of the walks are labelled ⓖ, and I recommend that anyone other than an *expert* walker hire a guide for these routes. This is because some areas are prone to sudden thick mists, making it easy to get lost on a mountain; or

because the path is hazardous, or difficult to distinguish, due to the lack of good waymarking.

Guides are not easily found on Mallorca, but you can enquire at Palma's Tourist Promotion Office, 1 Avenida Constitución. Alternatively, you can write in advance or telephone to Mauricio Espinar, Calle Almirante Cervera 23, Puerto de Pollensa (Tel: 531030). He can guide you over any part of the island; he speaks fluent English and French and understands some German.

Waymarking of walks is minimal. There is no signposting, but many of the mountain routes have been marked with red paint in years past (often hard to follow today). Another form of waymarking you'll see on the more difficult mountain routes is a small pile of stones — after a while, you'll become accustomed to keeping a look out for these unusual mountain 'signs'.

The **maps** in this book have been heavily adapted from 1:50,000 and 1:25,000 military maps of the island. These are available at the 'Armería', 7b Calle Arzobispo Aspargo, should you wish to pursue more walks. But do remember that, while they are useful for contours and heights, they are woefully out of date, and the routes shown may now be completely overgrown and dangerous — or privately owned.

R ight of way

Much of Mallorca's land is in private hands, and several landowners do try to discourage walkers by posting forbidding 'private' signs. There are no maps showing rights of way either. But, by law, walkers have right of way to: the coast, famous landmarks, *miradors*, monasteries and hermitages, towers and mountain peaks. You do have the right of way on all the routes described in this book, but should you encounter any difficulty with a landowner, do tell him just *where* you are going. See page 63, 'Meeting a landowner'.

Emerald-green waters of the Pareis Gorge at La Calobra (Picnic 9a)

What to take

If you're already on Mallorca when you find this book, and haven't any special equipment such as a rucksack, boots or a torch, you can still make some of the walks — or buy yourself some equipment at any of the sports shops in Palma. Don't attempt the more difficult walks without the proper equipment. For each walk in the book, the *minimum* equipment is listed. Where walking boots are required, there is, unfortunately, no substitute: you will need to rely on the grip and ankle support they provide, as well as their waterproof qualities. All other walks should be made with stout shoes, preferably with thick rubber soles, to grip on wet or slippery surfaces.

You may find the following checklist useful:

comfortable walking boots	up-to-date timetables (page 7)
waterproof rain gear	plastic bottle, purifying tablets
long-sleeved shirt (sun protection)	long trousers, tight at the ankles
bandages, plasters, etc	sun cream, insect repellant
plastic plates, cups, etc	knives, openers, string
anorak, two light cardigans	map (see page 55)
extra pair of socks, spare laces	sunhat, plastic rainhat
small rucksack	torch, whistle, compass
plastic groundsheet	first-aid kit, safety pins, etc

Please bear in mind that I've not made every walk in this book under *all* weather conditions, and I may not realise just how hot — or wet — some walks might be. The sun may be your worst enemy. It's tempting to walk in shorts and to forget that, with the sun behind you, the backs of your

The C713 south of Alaró is one of the most beautiful stretches of road on Mallorca. The foreground varies according to the time of year. You may pass by silvery olive trees or scarlet poppies, golden barley or pink almond blossoms. One of the most splendid sights on the road is the pass just north of Alaró, shown in the photograph at the left and on page 97. In both photographs, the sheer escarpments of the Puig de Alaró (on the left) and S'Alcanada (right) frame the northern sierra.

neck and legs are being badly burned. *Always* carry a long-sleeved shirt and long trousers to put on when you've had enough sun, and *always* wear a sunhat on bright days. It's a good idea as well to cover yourself generously with a protective sun cream. In hot weather, take your lunch in a shaded spot. Your good judgement will help you to modify the equipment list according to the season.

Weather
The weather on Mallorca can be quite variable. It can be very cold in winter — but not necessarily so. In fact, some winters are pleasantly mild. It is swelteringly hot and humid from July to September. The most unreliable months are March/April and September/October, when the capricious spring and autumn rains arrive.

Most people will find it far too hot in summer for any of the strenuous walks in this book. There are only two walks in the book which *must* be made in summer: Walk 8, from the Mirador de Ses Barques to La Calobra, relies on a boat connection from La Calobra, and this generally operates only between May and September. This walk is not too strenuous, especially if you omit the descent and return from Sa Costera. But there is very little shade; be sure to wear a sunhat and something covering your arms and the back of your neck and legs, and take plenty of water or fruit with you. Walk 9 (along the Torrente de Pareis) is only possible in summer, or after a long period without rain; it also relies on the La Calobra boat connection. At least you can cool yourself in the stream, and the shade from the towering cliffs provides some respite from the sun when it's not directly overhead.

Generally the best walking months are January and February — perhaps April, if it's not too wet, May and early June, September (likewise, if it's not too wet!), October, November and December. All lovers of mountainous islands, and certainly all walkers, will know that these rough guidelines are rules to which every year proves to be an exception — and freak weather, with heavy snow on the *sierra*, is not unknown in May!

A full weather report always appears, complete with meteorological maps, in the daily newspapers and on television every evening following the main news. For more information, you can telephone the 'Información Meteorológica' (Tel: 094) at any time of the day or night; be warned: the recorded message is in Spanish. Perhaps you can ask your hotel porter to interpret for you!

Dogs and other things that bite

You'll encounter **dogs** at all the farms, *almost* always chained up. It is a good idea for each walker always to carry a stout stick — to be used for self-protection; but when passing through a farm *never* wave the stick about to menace the dogs. Moreover, always go *quietly* through all private land, leaving gates *exactly* as you find them. Only resort to your stick when confronted by an unchained and obviously unfriendly dog.

There are four types of **snakes** on the island — some of the longest growing to about 1—1.5m (1—1½yds); none is dangerous to man. We also have **scorpions**, but these are tiny (4cm/1½in). Their bite might sting, but you won't come to any harm. More troublesome are **mosquitos** and **ticks**. Always carry insect repellant, and when walking in dense undergrowth, it's always wise to wear long trousers, with your socks pulled up round the trouser legs, and long sleeves.

Walkers' checklist

The following points cannot be stressed too often:

- **At any time a walk may become unsafe** due to heavy storms. If the route is not as described in this book, and your way ahead is not secure, do not attempt to go on.
- **Walks labelled Ⓖ** are generally unsuitable for winter walking, and the walks in the mountains *may* be very wet in winter — although not necessarily so.
- **Never walk alone** — four is the best walking group.
- **Do not overestimate your energies** — your speed will be determined by the slowest walker in your group.
- **Transport** connections at the end of a walk are vital.
- **Proper shoes or boots** are a necessity.
- **Mists** can suddenly appear on the higher mountains.
- **Warm clothing** is needed on the mountains; even in summer take some along, just in case you are delayed.
- **Compass, whistle, torch** weigh little, but might save your life.
- **Extra rations** must be taken on long walks.
- **Always take a sunhat** with you, and in summer a cover-up for your arms and legs as well.
- **A stout stick** is a help on rough terrain and to discourage the rare unchained, menacing dog.
- **Do not panic** in an emergency.
- **Read** and re-read the important note on page 2 and the country code on page 60, as well as guidelines on grade and equipment for each walk you plan to make.

Where to stay

Most people will be staying in or around Palma during their holiday on the island. From the capital a good public transport system permits daily travel to most parts of Mallorca. For this reason, all the walks are written up to include transport to and from Palma, where there is a wide selection of accommodation.

Whereas the capital is your best choice if you're relying on public transport, if you plan to rent a car you have a far greater choice of locations — especially if you plan only to make short or easy walks.

If you intend to do a lot of hiking, remember that most of the island's best — and most strenuous — walks lie along the mountain chain stretching from Valldemossa to Pollensa. Good centres for walks are therefore Sóller and its port and Pollensa and its port. This is especially so when the bus is running along the C710 mountain road between Sóller and Pollensa (see STOP PRESS, page 136); many of the walks then lie within easy reach.

Briefly, if you're planning to make a lot of walks, are *pre-booking a package holiday*, and will rely on public transport, **Palma** is your best centre. **Pollensa** and **Sóller** are also good choices, especially if the C710 bus is running.

For those *not* booking 'all-in' holidays, there is the interesting alternative of staying at one of Mallorca's sanctuaries, many of which still run a hostelry.

Lluc, a large monastery, steeped in history and set in romantic surroundings high in the mountains, is placed just at the centre of some of the best island walks. Visitors may stay overnight — or for as long as they wish — in the hostelry run by the friars. A bus service connects Lluc with Inca, from where there are hourly trains to Palma — so there's no need to feel 'cut off from civilisation'. Moreover, if the bus is running along the C710 between Soller and Pollensa, passing by Lluc — see page 136 — this hostelry becomes even more appealing as a centre.

The next best base for hostelry accommodation is Pollensa, where a small sanctuary atop the **Puig de María** (Walk 18) offers modest and inexpensive accommodation in spotless rooms with breathtaking views. Several other sanctuaries take in visitors, among them the Ermita de la Victoria near Alcudia, the Ermita de la Trinidad near Valldemossa, the Monastery of Cura (Randa), the Sanctuary of San Salvador (Felanitx) and the Sanctuary of Montesión (Porreres).

Finally, don't forget that there is simple hostel accommodation atop the Puig de **Alaró** (see pages 56 and 97).

A country code for walkers and motorists

The experienced rambler is used to following a 'country code' on his walks, but the tourist out for a lark may unwittingly cause damage, harm animals, and even endanger his own life. A code for behaviour is important wherever people roam over the countryside, but especially so on Mallorca — where you often cross private land, and where the rugged terrain can lead to dangerous mistakes.

palm bush

- **Only light fires** at picnic areas with fireplaces. Stub cigarettes out with care.
- **Do not frighten animals.** The goats and sheep you may encounter on your walks are not tame. By making loud noises or trying to touch or photograph them, you may cause them to run in fear and be hurt.
- **Walk quietly through all farms** and take care not to provoke the dogs. Ignore their barking and keep your walking stick out of their sight — remember, it is only to be shown to an unfriendly, *unchained* dog.
- **Leave all gates just as you found them**, whether they are at farms or on the mountainside. Although you may not see any animals, the gates *do* have a purpose — generally to keep goats or sheep in — or out of — an area. Here again, animals could be endangered by careless behaviour.
- **Protect all wild and cultivated plants.** Don't try to pick wild flowers or uproot saplings. They will die before you even get back to your hotel. Obviously fruit and other crops are someone's private property and should not be touched. **Never** walk over cultivated land.
- **Take all your litter back to the hotel with you.**
- **DO NOT TAKE RISKS!** This is the most important point of all. Do not attempt walks beyond your capacity, and do not wander off the paths described if there is any sign of mist or if it is late in the day. **Do not walk alone**, and **always** tell a responsible person — perhaps your hotel porter — *exactly* where you are going and what time you plan to return. Remember, if you become lost or injure yourself, it may be a long time before you are found. On any but a very short walk near to villages, be sure to take a compass, whistle, torch, extra water and warm clothing — as well as some high-energy food, like chocolate.

Organisation of the walks

The twenty-five rambles in the book are grouped in three general areas. Walks 1—7 are easily reached from Palma, by public transport, in an hour or less. Walks 8—16 radiate from the northern mountain route, the C710 (see **STOP PRESS**, page 136). Walks 17—25 are centred on the Pollensa—Artá axis and the bays of Pollensa and Alcudia.

I hope that the book is set out so that you can plan your walks easily — depending on how far you want to go, your abilities and equipment, and the season.

You might begin by considering the large colour fold-out map between pages 18 and 19. Here you can see at a glance the overall terrain, the road network, and the exact orientation of the walking maps in the text. Quickly flipping through the book, you'll find that there's at least one photograph for every walk.

Having selected one or two potential excursions from the map and the photographs, turn to the relevant walk. At the top of the page you'll find planning information: distance/hours, grade, equipment, and how to get there by public transport. If the grade and equipment specifications are beyond your scope, don't despair! *There's always at least one short version of each walk*, and in most cases these are far less demanding of agility and equipment!

When you are on your walk, you will find that the text begins with an introduction to the overall landscape and then quickly turns to a detailed description of the route itself. The large-scale maps (all to scale 1:50,000) have been specially annotated and set out facing the walking notes wherever possible. Times are given for reaching certain key checkpoints. Giving times is always tricky, because they depend on so many factors, but the times given fall in the range 2.4—3km per hour, depending on the terrain. Note that these times **include only minimal stops** — to catch your breath or take a photo. Be sure to allow extra time for other breaks — picnicking, swimming, sunbathing.

Many of the symbols used on the walking maps are self-explanatory, but here is a key to the most important ones:

▬ red roads on the colour map	corresponds to	�608 *canaleta* (p127)
	∞∞∞ tunnel	⊞ *atalaya* (p126)
═══ corresponds to white roads on the colour map	2▬ walk (in green)	♠/♣ monastery/*ermita*
	⊡ best views	♣ church or chapel
═══ track or trail	620 height (m)	⊡/⊠ castle/in ruins
--- path or steps	♠ danger— vertigo	**A** reference points for short and alternative walks
+++ railway	Ⓖ guide (p54)	**B**
		P picnics (see p10)

Spanish and Mallorquín

While Spanish is the official language of Mallorca, most of the islanders speak Mallorquín amongst themselves. And the island, like many other regions around the world, has an active minority of citizens who would prefer to re-establish Mallorquín as the official language. This linguistic 'tug-of-war' manifests itself in many ways.

You will notice that spellings of place names vary between maps and signposts — for example 'Andraitx' and 'Andratx'. Similarly, both the Spanish form La Calobra and the Mallorquín Sa Calobra are seen.

Those of us who live on Mallorca use both languages interchangeably — hardly noticing the discrepancies that are so obvious to confused visitors. Rather than use either Spanish or Mallorquín in this book, I have adopted the spellings in most common usage on the island today and have tried to be consistent.

Language hints for walkers and picnickers

In the tourist centres you'll find that almost everyone speaks at least a little English. But once out in the country-side, a few words of Spanish will be helpful, especially if you lose your way.

Here's an — almost — foolproof way to communicate in Spanish. First, memorise the few short key questions and their possible answers, given on the next page. Then, when you have your 'mini-speech' memorised, always ask the many questions you can concoct from it **in such a way that you get a 'sí' (yes) or 'no' answer.** Never ask an open-ended question such as 'Where is the main road?' You won't understand the answer — especially as it's likely to be given in Mallorquín! Instead, ask the question and then *suggest the most likely answer yourself.* For instance: 'Good day, sir. Please — where is the road to Lluc? *Is it straight ahead?*' Now, unless you get a '*sí*', try: '*Is it to the left?*' If you go through the list of answers to your own question, you will eventually get a '*sí*' response — probably with a vigorous nod of the head — and this is just that bit more reassuring than relying solely on sign language.

> An inexpensive phrase book, such as one of those published by Collins, Berlitz, or Penguin, is a very valuable aid, from which you may choose other 'key' phrases and answers.

Following are three of the most likely situations in which you may have to practice some Spanish. The dots (...) show where you will fill in the name of your destination. The correct pronunciation of place names will be found in the index, on pages 133-135.

Asking the way

The key questions

English	Spanish	pronounced as
Good day, sir (madam, miss).	Buenos días, señor (señora, señorita).	Boo-eh-nas dee-ahs, sen-yor (sen-yor-ah, sen-yor-ee-tah).
Please – where is	Por favor – dónde está	Poor fah-vor – dohn-day es-tah
the road to ... ?	la carretera a ... ?	lah cah-reh-teh-rah ah ...?
the footpath to ... ?	la senda de ... ?	lah sen-dah day ...?
the way to ... ?	el camino a ... ?	el cah-mee-noh ah ...?
the bus stop?	la parada de autobus?	lah pah-rah-dah day ow-toh-boos?
Many thanks.	Muchas gracias.	Moo-chas gra-thee-as.

Possible answers

English	Spanish	pronounced as
here	aquí	ah-kee
straight ahead	todo recto	toh-doh rec-toh
behind	detrás	day-tras
to the right	a la derecha	ah lah day-reh-chah
to the left	a la izquierda	ah lah eeth-kee-er-dah
above	arriba	ah-ree-bah
below	abajo	ah-bah-hoh

Asking a taxi driver to return for you

English	Spanish	pronounced as
Please –	Por favor	Poor fah-vor
take us to ...	llévanos a ...	l-yay-vah-nos ah ...
and return	y volver	ee vol-vair
for us at ...	para nosotros a ...	pah-rah nos-oh-tros ah ...

(Instead of memorising hours of the day, simply point out the time when you wish him to return on your watch, and get his agreement.)

Meeting a landowner who denies you access

See notes on page 55 about right of way. If you believe that you have right of way, you might ask:

English	Spanish	pronounced as
We are going to ...	Nos vamos a ...	Nos vah-mos ah ...
If this way	Si este camino	See es-tay cah-mee-noh
is private,	es privado,	es pree-vah-doh,
please –	por favor –	poor fah-vor –
show us	muéstranos	moo-es-trah-nos
the way.	el camino.	el cah-mee-noh.
Many thanks.	Muchas gracias.	Moo-chas grath-ee-as.

Once in a while you may meet people who do not speak Spanish. Greet them in Mallorquín and then pronounce *very carefully* the name of the place you are looking for (see Index for pronunciation of landmarks in this book). The Mallorquín for 'Good morning' is *Bon día* (**Bone dee**-ah); 'Good afternoon' is *Bonas tardas* (**Bone**-ahs **tar**-dahs).

1 SAN TELMO · CA'N TOMEVI · LA TRAPA · LA TORRE DE CALA BASET · SAN TELMO

Distance: 8km/4¾mi; about 3h

Grade: fairly easy, but it is an uphill climb most of the way to La Trapa, with some scrambling over rocks; path undefined at times

Equipment: walking boots, anorak, sunhat, picnic, water, torch

How to get there: 🚌 to Andraitx, but see NB below
Depart Palma 07.10 and every 45 minutes thereafter until 19.30; arrive Andraitx one hour later
Taxi from Andraitx to San Telmo
To return: taxi from San Telmo to Andraitx
🚌 from Andraitx to Palma
Departs Andraitx every 45min from 07.30 to 19.30; journey time 1h
NB: On Sundays *only*, there is a bus from Palma direct to San Telmo and return; dep Palma 09.00; dep San Telmo 17.15; journey time 1½h

Short walk: A→B→C→A takes in some highlights and avoids the climb to La Trapa: 3.5km/2mi; 1¼h. Follow the main walk, but at Ca'n Tomeví, turn left by a pine tree, *before* the path to La Trapa. From here, follow the notes in the last three paragraphs on page 66

A bout seven kilometres along the winding country road from Andraitx, the peaceful and picturesque summer resort of San Telmo reclines on the south coast, looking out across the stretch of deep blue waters towards the rocky island of Sa Dragonera. There are many pretty woodland walks in this area, but by far the most interesting is a visit to the ruins of the ancient Trappist monastery, some 380m/ 1250ft up on the rocky cliffside, facing out towards the distant Spanish mainland. This low stretch of pine-covered coastline is also the home of a variety of birds, including red kites, rock sparrows, and alpine swifts.

Any season permits a walk on this headland, but avoid the climb to La Trapa in summer. On cool days, remember to take warm clothing: the fresh winds coming off the sea can make it very chilly up at the monastery ruins.

From the bus stop in San Telmo, continue west along the coast road (PM103), crossing the bridge. You'll come to a large *plaza* (some 800m beyond the bus stop), and this is where **the walk begins.** Follow the road leading from the plaza towards the pine woods, passing some chalets (on your right, you'll see a bar near a windmill). The asphalt soon ends; continue along the earthen track and you'll come to Ca'n Tomeví in **15min.** There's an old winehouse here, where you can fortify yourself for the climb to come!

From Ca'n Tomeví take the path straight ahead, following the red arrow painted on a pine tree by a clearing. Pass a sandstone quarry on your left, and start to climb. Cross a track (a left turn here leads to the pretty cove of Cala Baset) and continue straight on, beside a barbed-wire fence.

There is a red 'T' painted on a tree. From here on the path is sometimes hard to distinguish. Climb up, rounding the headland, with good views of Sa Dragonera and Sa Pantaleu, a large rock jutting up out of the sea. Higher up, where the trees have thinned out, you'll have to scramble over some rocks, and when you reach what seems to be the top of the cliff, keep a very sharp watch for the red arrows that point to the right, where the path climbs over some large rocks and boulders. If you miss this, you will come to a rather precipitous edge. Once over the brow of the cliff, you will be able to see the ruins of the monastery ahead. The going is a lot easier now: the path runs alongside the coastline, through more pines, and descends gently. About 150m (yds) before La Trapa, you'll see a path leading off to the right; it crosses the brow of the mountain and descends in U-bends back to Ca'n Tomeví (an easy alternative route back, if you do not wish to visit Cala Baset).

La Trapa is set back from the cliff edge on a series of grassy, sloping terraces, right by the side of an enormous *ombu* tree. Trappist monks lived here until the end of the

Windswept pines on the San Telmo headlands; the isle of Dragonera (not seen in the photograph) is off to the right (Picnic 1)

The foothills around Esporles (Picnic 2)

eighteenth century, when the Spanish government abolished many of these institutions for both political and financial reasons. Recently, it has come under the protection of the Balearic Ornithological Group, who hope to keep this land safe from the ever-encroaching tentacles of *la urbanización*. Walk on round, past the monastery and the lovely almond tree-planted terrace, where the remains of an old mill face across to the ruins. If you continue on to the *mirador*, be careful of the steep drops to the sea. Back past the old mill, you can explore the neat stone steps that lead from one terrace to another and find the old well, or fountain, hiding at the end of a tunnel — if you brought a torch. There are several good spots for picnicking — including inside the ruins, should you get caught in a shower!

The way back is by the same route, until you re-reach Ca'n Tomeví (**2h**). Here turn right at the pine tree by the open clearing and follow the sandy track. Keep left five minutes on, going alongside a wire fence, following the red daubs on the trees. Meet another track crossing at right angles, but keep straight on and climb steadily, with good views of San Telmo's bay. Soon the track ends, but we follow the small path ahead, passing a ruined stone hut, and a minute later come out onto a wide track. Here turn up right. Five minutes later, the wide track ends; follow the red arrow pointing right along the main trail through the trees. Pass through two small clearings and, keeping left, arrive at the Torre de Cala Baset (**2h30min**).

You can climb the iron rungs to the lookout on top, from where you will see the rocky cove of Cala Baset below on your right and, to the left, over the water, Sa Dragonera, with its own *atalaya* on the top-most point of the island.

Go back along the same route, this time simply following the wide main track, which leads back to San Telmo (**3h**).

2 ESPORLES · NA BOSCANA · ESPORLES

Distance: 9km/5½mi; 3½h   See photograph opposite

Grade: not difficult, but there is a climb of 350m/1200ft

Equipment: stout shoes, sunhat, cardigan, picnic, water

How to get there: 🚌 to Esporles (journey time 30min)
Summer: dep 10.00; *winter:* dep 12.00 Mo—Fri, 09.00 Sat, 10.00 Sun
To return: 🚌 from Esporles to Palma (journey time 30min)
Summer: dep 15.30; *winter:* dep 18.40 (weekdays), 15.00 (Sat—Sun)

Short walk (only possible if you have a car): from Son Ferrá to the
mirador (A→B→A: 3km/1¾mi; 1¼h *return*); a climb of 200m/650ft.
Equipment as above. Park well 'tucked in' by the Son Ferrá gates

A midst undulating hills and valleys, where olive trees, almonds and carobs abound, a small country lane winds its way up from the centre of Esporles towards the *finca* of Son Ferrá, from where an old footpath climbs the wooded slopes of Na Boscana up to a *mirador* and an *ermita*.

The walk begins at the signpost to 'Es Verger'. Follow the country lane gradually uphill for about **40min**, keeping a lookout for a wooden gate on your right, where the word 'Ermita' is painted in red on a stone wall. (The gate is about 50m (yds) below the gates to Son Ferrá, so even if you miss it, you can quickly return.)

Join the wide path behind the gate to start the fairly steep climb. In **1h25min** you'll reach a small clearing, where a yellow signpost shows the way to 'Monumento' up right — the *mirador* and its monument to Christ — a ten-minute walk from here. Cross a *sitja* and soon come to the viewpoint, from where the panorama will hold you enthralled. Esporles lies below in the valley, between pine-covered hills, with the higher mountains of the Sierra de Tramuntana behind, and the rolling countryside sweeping down to where the city of Palma cradles the wide blue bay.

From here it's a climb of 15 minutes more, should you wish to visit the (closed) *ermita*, before you make your leisurely descent back to Esporles. If you have time, the northern entrance to the village is exceptionally pretty, and you might like to visit the thirteenth-century church.

3 BUNYOLA · MIRADOR LEANDRO XIMENIS

Left: Bunyola's terraced olive trees (Picnic 3)

Distance: 9km/5½mi; about 3¾h

Grade: not difficult, but a climb of about 400m/1300ft

Equipment: stout shoes, sunhat, cardigan, picnic, water

How to get there: Sóller 🚃 to Bunyola Depart Palma 08.00, 10.40, 13.00, 15.15; arrive Bunyola 20min later
To return: 🚃 from Bunyola to Palma Departures at 12.15, 14.35, 18.45

Short walk: as far as you like along the path of the main walk; A→B takes under 1¼h *return* and affords good views with little climbing

O live trees and terraces, with sweeping views of the *sierras* are an early reward on this walk, easily reached from Bunyola station. **Start out** by turning left down the country road, to join the main C711. Here turn right, pass by the restaurant Ca'n Penasso and continue for 800m/yds, to find the sign to 'Alquería d'Avall' on the left (**30min**), where the route to a *mirador* atop the Alquería peak begins.

Turn up left to the farmhouse, taking the first left just before the buildings, and going through the black iron gates. The guard dog here is extremely menacing, and his chain is long; you can squeeze by just to the left of him. If you carry a stout stick (keep it at your side — do *not* threaten him), he will stay well clear of you. After you've gone through two more sets of gates, you'll find a lovely picnic spot, on the first S-bend, overlooking olive groves — just out of view of the farmhouse. Then enjoy good views of Bunyola, before the track plunges deep into woodlands.

Still keeping to the main track, zig-zag up the shaded mountainside, passing some old wells and shelters, until at about **1h40min** you reach a level area. Here, as the track bends to the left through trees, find the worn stone steps to the *mirador.* Twenty minutes more, along a narrow, climbing path will bring you to the viewpoint, where you'll find splendid vistas, an old shelter, a well and a fireplace.

Allow somewhat over an hour and a half for the return to Bunyola's station from here. Perhaps sample some of the local liqueur, *palo,* before boarding the 'wild-west' train for the return to Palma.

© 1987 SUNFLOWER BOOKS

68

4 SANTA EUGENIA · SES COVES · PUIG D'EN MARRON · SANTA EUGENIA

Distance: 7.5km/4½mi; under 2¾h

Grade: easy — moderate ascents

Equipment: stout shoes, sunhat, picnic, water, mosquito repellant

How to get there: 🚌 to Santa Eugenia; ask for 'Ses Coves'
Depart Palma 13.30 Mon—Sat, 9.00 Sundays; arrive 35min later
To return: 🚌 from Santa Eugenia (outside the school) to Palma
Departs 15.15; arrives Palma 15.45; departs 18.00 Sundays/holidays

Short walk: A→B→C (Plaza España to cross monument, down
through pass between boulders (see page 12, Picnic 4), turn
left at foot of the hill, and return to Santa Eugenia by the Camino
de las Ollerías: 2.5km/1½mi; under 1h); easy climb of 100m/325ft

E njoy this delightful country walk at any time of year.
The Puig d'en Marron is covered in pines, and the caves
hiding in the hillsides contain silent memories of the past.

Having asked the bus driver for 'Ses Coves', **begin the
walk** by following the narrow country lane up right into the
rocky hills. (If you come by car, leave it in Santa Eugenia
and walk to this lane — 15min northwest of the village on
the main road (PM104); the lane is then on your *left*.)

In **20min** you'll come to a bend in the road, where an
old abandoned stone well sits. Be sure not to take the track
leading off to the right here, but continue on up the road,
passing by the gnarled and ancient olive tree. Now the old
stone houses of Ses Coves (the caves) gradually come into
view, silently looking out over the plain through a maze of
pricky-pear cacti. Soon you'll catch your first view of the
caves themselves. In the biggest of these is an old wine-press.
This ancient-looking object was last used in the early 1920s,
and behind the mysterious wooden door, half hidden by
the undergrowth, are the dark, cool wine cellars, where the
enormous vats are still stored away, forgotten. The hills
here are riddled with many other caves, where pirates used
to store their smuggled goods, and which were also used as
dwelling-places by the Moors hundreds of years ago.

At **25min** the road divides in two; take the turning left.
At **30min** you'll come to some wide iron gates. This is the
entrance to the *puig*. Once through the gates, your uphill
climb begins. In spring, the beautiful song of the nightingale
is the only sound that echoes in the pine-scented silence.
You will see hoopoes, and wild rabbits scurrying into the
undergrowth, as your footsteps disturb their peace.

At **50min** the road ends, dividing into two tracks. It is
not possible to get lost on this small mountain, if you
always keep to the right along the main track. (The track
straight ahead takes you through tall pines to the south side

of the mountain, with some superb views of the southeast part of the island and the distant airport with its ribbon-like runways. It is also possible to descend the mountain here, by turning left onto the Camino de las Ollerías and following down into Santa Eugenia.)

But we turn right; the trees thin out in about 15 minutes, giving way to a large open space which covers the brow of the mountain. Up here, a good deal of the island may be seen. Turn left, following alongside the line of trees, in the direction of a square stone monument: now the magnificent mountain range stretches out before you along the west coast, with Es Pla (the plain) immediately before you. The town of Inca and Palma city are visible, as well as so many other towns and hamlets dotting the landscape. Explore the open tableland to find the best vantage points, and then find a good spot to picnic — you'll be an item of some interest to the inquisitive mountain goats wandering about!

To start down the mountain, follow the same route until you reach the gates guarding the *puig*. Once in the valley again, turn right, in the opposite direction from which you came, following the tarmac path. Pass by the ancient Arab burial ground, set back on the slopes at the left. While to the casual observer it is simply a mound of rocks and boulders, covered with prickly-pear cactus, excavations here in the early 1900s revealed human bones and relics dating back to the eighth and tenth centuries, when the Moors invaded and settled on the island.

About 150m (yds) past the burial grounds, ignoring the first left-hand cart track, take the sandy cart track to the left. Pass a gated, arched entrance to an old well and take the first left turn past the well, on a sandy track, heading for the cross monument. This track ends at a chalet. At its right, find the gap in the stone wall (marked with a vertical red paint daub) and climb an easily-seen footpath. As you climb, the cross monument will be on your left and a strange-looking 'UFO'-type object on your right. It's

The plain and and northern sierra, from the Puig de Santa Eugenia (Picnic 4)

really an old sea-craft, now converted into a weekend hideaway.

We soon approach a pass: just before it, there's a rocky platform between two boulders. This is a good place to admire the view — good also for picnicking, because it's protected from the winds that harass the plain. As soon as you clamber up between the boulders, the winds which usually blow straight across the plain will catch at your clothing and sting your cheeks. This is an exhilarating moment, as you look down on Es Pla, with the tang of the sea blowing on the wind. Now climb over the stone wall at the left, and make for the cross monument, from where almost all of the island is visible. Back down on the main path, turn left past a large, gnarled pine, through low scrub, until at **2h30min** you come to a rough, walled-in, stony track, barred by a locked gate. There is a gap in the wall, through which you can scramble, to continue on down to Santa Eugenia, easily seen and just ten minutes from here.

5 VALLDEMOSSA · MIRADOR DE SES PUNTES · CAMINO DEL ARCHIDUQUE · EL TEIX

Distance: 14km/8½mi; 6½h
Grade: strenuous. **G** for the climb from the Mirador de Ses Puntes up to the *meseta*, where the paths are not always easy to find and there is a danger of sudden thick mists falling and a danger of vertigo
Equipment: walking boots, long trousers, picnic, water, whistle, cardigans, compass; in winter anorak, hat, gloves, extra food
How to get there: 🚌 to Valldemossa
Depart Palma 10.00; arrive Valldemossa 10.30 *winter*; in *summer* there is an earlier departure at 07.45; arrives Valldemossa 08.15
To return: 🚌 from Valldemossa to Palma
Departs 16.00, 18.30 *winter*; departs 15.30, 17.00, 19.30 *summer*; journey time ½h
Short walks: no guide required for either; both are strenuous, Short walk 1 the more so; picnic, water, sunhat, extra clothing in winter

1   Valldemossa to the Mirador de Ses Puntes and return (A→B→A: 6km/3¾mi; 2½h); follow course of main walk and return same way

2   Valldemossa to ICONA shelter below El Teix (A→C→A: 6km/ 3¾mi; 2½h); go right on road *in front of* Son Gual; when it turns off right in a hairpin bend, fork left up track; stout shoes will suffice

Alternatives: Combine Short walk 2 with a climb to El Teix (+1½h); descend from El Teix to the Coll de Sóller (1½h) or Sóller (3½h)

O ne of the island's best walks, boasting splendid views *and* much historical interest. Moreover, it offers so many permutations that any walker with energy can tackle a suitable *part* of the walk, depending on the season. The main route follows a trail up into the thickly-wooded mountains near Valldemossa, joins the Camino del Archiduque, rounds the edge of the high plateau with its fantastic coastal views (and exciting sheer drops!), climbs and scrambles up to the summit of El Teix, and then drops back down to Valldemossa through the pretty Cairats Valley.

Start the walk at the bus stop in Valldemossa. From the *parada* walk back up the main (Palma) road (the way the bus has just come). You'll soon spot a very large old house with a tower — Son Gual — on the left. Turn left up the road before the house, and then take your first right. Left again before the house (unless you are doing Short walk 2 — in which case continue on *past* Son Gual). From here continue straight uphill, through this fairly new housing estate, until you come to the top of the hill, by a lovely stone wall. Here there is a sign on a lamppost, referring to various landmarks on our route. Turn left, then curve right round a large house. Here turn left up a track and follow it towards the beautiful group of umbrella pines. Just before you reach the pines, turn left up a stony path (**20min**), marked with a red paint daub.

Soon reach an old broken gate which you must climb; then continue ahead for about five minutes more, passing by two woodcutters' trails, until you see the red arrow painted on a rock at a bend, pointing up to the right. Pass a *sitja* on the left at **40min**; just past here, fork right and fork right again a few minutes later. In **50min** come to a 'cross-roads': go straight ahead to pass an old stone oven on the left. You'll soon meet a stone wall, where, again, you will have to climb over a gate (**1h**). Just beyond you'll reach level ground — an extensive and shaded open area — a good spot to take a quick rest. In this clearing, you'll see tracks left and right. But go straight ahead to find two forks out of the clearing: opt for the left hand one, and cross over a *sitja*. In **1h5min** you'll pass the well of Es Pouet (the water is *not* fit to drink). Soon the path begins to climb again, with the high, pine- and oak-wooded rocky mountain of Veyá on your right. At about **1h15min** you'll pass another *sitja*, and, just beyond it, another old stone oven.

Soon you glimpse the sea, and, forking left towards the *mirador*, there are excellent views of the coast. It's ten minutes more to the Mirador de Ses Puntes, from where you can see down the western coastline almost as far as Bañalbufar — if swirling mists don't play tricks on you!

Turn right from the *mirador* to follow the famous Camino del Archiduque, a stone-laid trail which climbs the Veyá mountain, dips into the valley of S'Estret de Son Gallart, and then climbs again onto the high plateau.

About twenty minutes along from the *mirador*, take the path to the left, following the (infrequent) splashes of red paint. At **1h45min** climb a rocky slope to a trigonometric stone. As you continue straight ahead through the woods, notice how the branches of the trees are covered with a thick, lichen-type green moss, due to the humidity of the frequent mists that swirl around the mountaintops.

Overlook Valldemossa from beneath these umbrella pines (Picnic 5)

At **1h55min** climb up to an abandoned stone shelter, from where there are more magnificent views. Go straight down the opposite side of the shelter, keeping a sharp look-out for the small rock-piles and *very* sparse red paint daubs. At **2h5min** take the fork to the right; the left-hand turning leads to Deiá. Ten minutes later, you will arrive at a 'cross-roads' in the valley, the Coll de S'Estret de Son Gallart. The path down right leads back to Es Pouet and the one left also to Deiá. Our *camino* continues in front. Standing on the rocks

Sólle

Lluc-Alcari

Son Marroig

Deiá

N

0

N

710

Miramar

Valldemossa

© 1987 SUNFLOWER BOOKS

2km

Mirador
de Ses
Puntes

Coll de
Sólle

Coll de S'Estret de
Son Gallart

910

G

B

867

762

Camino del Archiduque

Teix
1063

696

Veyá

Font d'es Pouet

874

Fontanellas

Font
d'es
Polls

ICONA

Es Caragol

Cairats

P

710

111

Son Gual

Palma

408

VALLDEMOSSA

here, you can see the distant bay of Sóller and the pretty mountain village of Deiá (see also page 24). Notice as well the strange tree formations down the immediate slopes — deliberately cultivated this way for thrush-netting.

Now continue ahead, pass a gap in the old stone wall and come to a rest area with stone seats. From here, an easily-followed path leads right down to Es Pouet. Our way passes to the right of the seats and begins its steep 20-minute climb to the high plateau. Once up on the *meseta*, you can see forever! There are splendid views on all sides. Right down the coastline, Galatzó pushes its peak through the scudding clouds. Deiá lies hundreds of feet below — also the famous Foradada (the rock pierced with a hole), that juts out into the sea near Son Marroig. The Bay of Sóller reposes peace-fully under the Mediterranean sun, and to the south, Palma's bay glistens like a huge round mirror, with the high cliffs of Cabo Blanco on the horizon. But this path skirts the edge of the plateau, with very precipitous drops to the left: go with a guide and be *extra* vigilant along here if it's misty!

At about **3h5min**, just by a small group of pines, a pile of rocks on the right indicates another way back to Es Pouet. Continue towards the sparsely-grouped trees ahead, where you might stop and picnic in the company of sheep and rosemary-scented air.

When you renew your journey, the peak of El Teix soon beckons (**3h45min**). It looks deceptively near, but it will take us about an hour and a half to get to the top and re-turn. The rewards are never-to-be-forgotten views of almost the entire island from the summit at 1063m/3500ft!

Returning from the Teix, rejoin the rocky path which begins its decent into the Cairats Valley. Soon you'll come to a snow pit and, at about **5h30min** — having met a new, wider track — you will arrive at the ICONA shelter. This is an ideal resting place, with a large fireplace and wooden tables and benches. From here down to the end of the walk, you'll find that ICONA has signposted several exam-ples of the Mallorcan customs described on pages 126 to 129.

Some eight minutes below the shelter, you'll pass the Font d'es Polls (the Poplars' Well). If you're doing Short walk 2 or the Alternative walk, you may have time to tackle the steep path here, leading up the cliffside of Es Caragol. After **6h** walking come to a first gate; meet a second gate ten minutes on. Soon the track ends and you find a curving tarmac road. Fork right here, and follow the road to the front of Son Gual (**6h30min**).

6 PUERTO DE SOLLER · S'ILLETA

See MAP on reverse of touring map
Distance: 9km/5½mi; 3¼h   Grade: easy climb
Equipment: stout shoes, picnic, sunhat, water
How to get there: any convenient train to Sóller and tram to the port
Short walk: from the port to the Torre Picada and return (A→B→A:
5km/3mi; 1¾h); easy, but you *do* have a climb of 150m/495ft

L a Torre Picada, a seventeenth-century watchtower atop
the hill called Sa Punta Grossa, commands very fine
views of Puerto de Sóller and the surrounding rocky coast.
For further adventure, you can follow the trail along the
coast as far as S'Illeta and admire the wild and rugged panorama of rocky mountains and deep blue sea.

Start out at the Altamar snack bar, south of the tram/bus
stops. Turn uphill, and then cross the streambed by going
left over the bridge. Now turn right: this road becomes the
Carrer de Bélgica and climbs up through a housing estate.
Where the road bends left, notice a small junction to the
right — this can be your return route. When the road
divides in two (**25min**), turn up right by the block of flats.
After about 100m (yds), the road comes to an end at a gate.
Pass through the access gate on the right and follow the
stony track until at **45min**, you come to a fork; from here
it's five minutes up left to the *atalaya*. The tower is closed
to prevent further damage by vandals, but there are excellent views all round. The rocky islet of S'Illeta is visible to
the north, and the small headland of Ses Puntes below.

Back at the fork, the track winds down through the
woods and comes to a flat area, with a gate and stile over
the wall. To continue on to S'Illeta, it is best to get over the
stile and turn left up the hard track on the other side,
continuing along the coast as far as possible, until the path
ends opposite S'Illeta (**1h50min**). The wild landscape along
here offers untold opportunities for keen photographers!

*Approaching the Torre Picada (Picnic 6). See the tower from a
different perspective in the photograph on page 27*

7 SOLLER · BINIARAIX · ES BARRANC · FINCA DE L'OFRE · ES CORNADORS · S'ARROM · SOLLER

Distance: 16km/9¾mi; 7h   See MAP on reverse of touring map

Grade: strenuous, but along clearly defined paths most of the way. The ascent of 900m/2950ft is tiring

Equipment: stout walking shoes or boots, cardigan, anorak, sunhat, picnic, water purifying tablets (or water in summer months)

How to get there: 🚂 to Sóller
Depart Palma 08.00; arrive Sóller 09.00 (there is another departure at 10.40, but the train is usually very crowded, and you would not have enough time to complete the long walk)
To return: 🚂 from Sóller to Palma
Departs Soller 14.10 and 18.20; arrives Palma one hour later (a later train departs Sóller 21.00 Sundays and *fiesta* days only)

Short walk: Sóller to Biniaraix (A→B) and on up the path of Es Barranc as far as you like for good views without too much climbing; it will take 1¼h from Sóller to Biniaraix *and return*; equipment as above; boots not necessary

Alternative walk: Cúber reservoir to Sóller (C→B→A; 12km/7¼mi; 4½h); easy, but steep descent to Biniaraix. Good track from Cúber

This is surely one of the most beautiful walks on the island! There are leafy glades, impressive cliff-sides, waterfalls, green valleys, rocky mountains, and magnificent views from the Mirador de l'Ofre — at 955m/3135ft, it's certainly worth the effort it takes to get there! Be sure to check the weather forecast before making this walk; it would be a shame to get all the way up to the *mirador*, only to find the Sóller valley covered in low-lying mists. The best time of year is a clear cool spring day.

The walk begins in the Plaça de Sa Constitució (map on page 27; photograph page 81). From here we follow a narrow street to the square in the tiny hamlet of Biniaraix, dominated by a large tree (**35min**). On the right, above the Calle de San José, is a signpost 'Lluc a pie'; this is the route we follow. A minute later, turn sharp right: you will see the footpath beginning straight ahead, signed 'Camí d'es Barranc'*. Some minutes later, pass a gate on the left with a 'no entry' sign on it. Continue to the right, following the red arrow and the words 'L'Ofre, Lluc a peu' (Lluc on foot).

*The Camí d'es Barranc is the first stage of an ancient pilgrims' way from Sóller to Lluc. We follow it as far as the Finca de l'Ofre. From there, the 16th-century way travelled north of the peaks of L'Ofre, Tossals and Massanella as far as Lluc. Walk 11 again touches on the old trail, at the Font d'es Prat. Today the way cannot be followed in its entirety, since the C710 has obliterated it near the Cúber Reservoir. The Alternative walk again takes up the trail between Cúber and Ofre's farm, on a good, easy track (2h). Around Massanella, the way is totally lost.

At about **45min** cross a small bridge — the first past Biniaraix — over the stream, and continue on up the stony steps. The rushing waters of the stream echo mystically around you . . . certainly a magical place, especially early in the morning as the mists are rising!

At **55min** follow the main path, ignoring the small stone steps that lead up to the right. Just past here, a rather impressive cliff-face looms up before you on the right. Soon cross a second bridge over this curious stream which rushes along quite noisily and then disappears underground, so that one moment you can hear the water cascading over the rocks, and then all of a sudden you notice how silent it is!

An old stone house, once used by the olive-pickers, appears just up ahead at **1h20min**, where the path turns to the left. At **1h45min** cross a third bridge, and soon a fourth and last bridge. A little further along, a fairly big house appears on the left, with a very neat stone wall surrounding it. Continue straight ahead here: you will see the word 'Lluc' painted in faded blue on the wall — also a big red arrow. (The path leading off to the left only goes to an ancient well in the mountains called Font d'es Verger.) Keep always to the main path, as one or two smaller ones appear on the right. At **2h** the main path takes a sharp turn to the left: be careful not to follow the flat earth path that leads on straight ahead of you.

It's a good idea to stop now and then from here on, not only to catch your breath, but to admire the scintillating views. The village of Sóller seems so far away now, and the lighthouse in the Bay of Sóller can also be seen. The cluster of houses at Biniaraix seems infinitely tiny — almost unreal.

As you proceed another fantastic cliff-face confronts you, full of holes in the rocks where falcons, wild pigeons and other birds have made their nests. A truly impressive waterfall cascades down this steep rock face after a heavy rainy season. Soon, a rugged deep ravine appears on the right, where the fury of the rushing waters echoes from far below. Just past here, you will come across the iron gates that guard the Finca de l'Ofre (**2h30min**). Don't be put off by the various signs — this is a public pathway, and you are quite at liberty to go through. Don't worry about the loose bulls wandering about here either; they're meek as lambs and terrified of humans! Painted on the brick walls of the farm building are clear indications of our route.

Our track is the one that leads off to the right, through the farm. Cross the flat area beyond a second, smaller farmhouse, to find the rocky mountain path to the Mirador de l'Ofre — which, confusingly enough, is on the Cornadors mountain! — straight ahead. (The peak of L'Ofre itself, on the trail to Lluc, soars up behind us at 1090m/3575ft.)

After 100m (yds), go through an old and rusty gate, where there is a rough sheep-hold just beyond on the right. Take a breather now, and turn to admire the high, silent Sierra of Alfabia on the left, together with the pretty valley and farmhouses below — a wonderful panorama.

Continue the stony ascent. If it's sunny, please wear a sunhat — there's no shade to be found until you reach the shelter at the top, and the sun is now quite high. You will pass by two unusual stone columns, formed by the wind, and climb a fence, aided by wooden hand-made ladders, until at **3h40min** you reach the point where the rocky pathway divides in two. Turning up to the right, the path leads you to the low stone shelter. Now, scramble across the rocks and boulders, over the brow of Es Cornadors, to find the fabulous *mirador*.

The views from here are truly breath-taking: the whole of the valley of Sóller lies like a miniature toy world far below you, and the fairy-tale villages of Biniaraix and Fornalutx appear like small blotches on a neat, green copybook. Beyond lies the distant Bay of Soller and all round the magnificence of the mountains: the Sierra de Alfabia, the Coll de Sóller, El Teix, the Puig Mayor, L'Ofre.

Return now, across the rocks and back to the shelter — a good place to have your picnic lunch. The shade offered by the stone building is quite welcome on a sunny day, and you can admire the views from the south side of Es Cornadors. After having your fill of food and views, return to where the rocky path divides into two, this time continuing on down to the right. At **4h** cross over the stone wall by means of the iron ladders that bypass the locked gate. Now you will find the path not nearly so rocky and uncomfortable, and the shade from the evergreens makes a welcome respite. Follow on, through these pleasantly cool, leafy glades, with nothing but the smell of pines and the distant chiming of the church bells of Sóller to accompany you. At **4h30min** a small grassy *sitja* appears on the left, and five minutes further along, you'll pass by a rusty iron gate

Overlooking the hamlet of Biniaraix from Es Barranc — the old pilgrims' trail to Lluc — the setting for Picnic ;

on the right, soon going through some broken old wooden gates. Soon now, small stone steps lead up left to an old spring, the Font de Ses Piquetes (best to use purifying tablets if you take on water here). The main path passes through another iron gate a few metres (yards) further along. About 100m (yds) past this gate, take a sharp turn to the right, where there is a small path leading downwards, just by the side of a large pine tree. The continuing path later doubles back to meet this narrower path further down, so there is no danger of getting lost! Continue on down the rough stone steps, and at the bottom turn right, past a big old farmhouse. Past the house, take the track to the left and continue through the farm of S'Arrom, passing through two sets of iron gates and following on down the wide, stony track. At about **5h10min**, just by a rough lean-to used as a car port, the way divides into two again. The left hand track through the gates just leads to the house; we go right and then swing round left through some gates behind the house. Five minutes later, take the turning to the left through more gates, where you will find the word 'Sóller' painted in blue on the rocky wall. Continue now, an easy descent, along a wide, winding track. At **6h** a tall iron gate with spikes on top is usually locked, but you can pass through the small access gate on the right. Five minutes later, the track is surfaced for about 100m, just by a large house. Soon a small bridge crosses the Torrente de Ca'n Miro, and a few minutes later, a second bridge. Pass through yet another double iron gate. More and more little houses keep popping up as you draw near to Sóller. Ignore the track off to the left and continue right, until at **6h30min** a wide bridge on your left crosses the stream, just by the side of an old stone *canaleta*. Turn right, down and away from the bridge, along the tarmac road and past the high-walled cemetery. Use the sketch map on page 27 to make your way to the station, where you will probably have time to sit with a drink in one of the bar-cafés before boarding the 'wild-west' train for your return to the capital.

The Plaça de Sa Constitució (Constitution Square), Sóller.
This is a nice place to have a relaxing break and watch the world go by, before boarding your train or tram

8 MIRADOR DE SES BARQUES · SA COSTERA · CALA TUENT · LA CALOBRA · SOLLER

Distance: 16km/9¾mi; 6h   **See MAP on reverse of touring map**

Grade: moderate, with several ascents and descents (all on good tracks/trails)

Equipment: stout walking shoes (boots outside summer months), sunhat, insect repellant, cardigans and anorak in cold weather, picnic, plastic bottle with water purifying tablets (water in summer)

How to get there: 🚆 to Sóller
Depart Palma 08.00; arrive Sóller 09.00. *Taxi from Sóller station to 'Mirador des Ses Barques';* but see also **STOP PRESS**, page 136
To return: ⛴ from La Calobra to Puerto de Soller (last departure 16.45; 🚌 from the port to Soller (dep 17.55) in time for the last 🚆 to Palma (dep 18.20 daily; a further departure 21.00 Sundays)
NB: The boat from La Calobra **only runs from May to September** and **will not take large groups.** If you are more than three or four, or if you make the walk outside summer, opt for the Alternative walk described below

Short walk: from the Mirador de Ses Barques as far as you like in the Bálitx valley, where you can picnic. Allow about one hour walking *return*, and be sure to ask the taxi driver to wait for you or to return for you (see page 63); stout shoes, sunhat, picnic, water

Alternative walk: Mirador de Ses Barques to Sa Costera and return (A→B→A: 12km/7¼mi; under 5h); grade and equipment as main walk. Ask the taxi to return to the viewpoint for you (see page 63)

T he Mirador de Ses Barques is one of the most scenic spots along this beautiful stretch of mountainous coastline near Sóller. From over 400 metres we can take in the magnificent panorama shown on page 27, with the village and port in the valley below, surrounded by the high *sierra,*

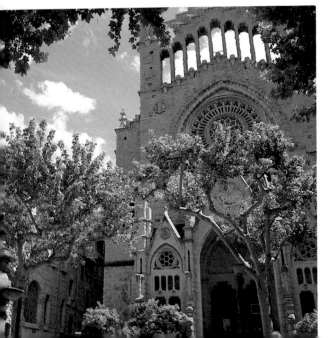

and the deep blue Mediterranean shimmering beneath in the sun. The *mirador* is also famous for its freshly squeezed orange juice, so why not enjoy a sparkling glassful of 'sunshine' before embarking on this hiking adventure?

The walk begins here at the viewpoint, just down on the right, past the piled-up crates of empty bottles, and through the open gates. The track is wide, flat and comfortable. Ignore all off-shoots and in **5min** you'll meet large green gates. Just past here, the artistically-cultivated terraced slopes, studded with a multitude of silvery-leaved olive trees, are especially picturesque. Soon you will be able to see the large old farmstead of Balitx de Dalt (Bálitx on the Heights) ahead on the hillside. When the path forks at **15min**, go right through the rusty gates and enter the incredibly beautiful valley of Bálitx, where the footpath winds away over the hills into the distance, through myriad olive groves. At **20min** a stony path straight ahead is a short-cut to the Font de Bálitx, where you'll find lovely fresh water outside summer months. (The path leading up the hillside from here is an old route to Montcaire, now closed to walkers.) The short-cut rejoins the track, and we pass by the abandoned farm of Bálitx d'en Midj (Middle Bálitx), now sadly in ruins. Sheep and pigs wander in and out in search of pastureland. Follow the track past the farm, and go through another rusty iron gate and then one more. Continue along the track as it meanders on down into the valley. From here you can see the ancient *atalaya* of Na Torre Seca up on the hilltop across the valley to the north.

In **1h** you will come to the farm of Bálitx de Baix (Lower Bálitx), where your approach will be heralded by the alert guard dogs, unaccustomed to frequent passers-by. Here, just before the farm buildings, turn down towards the right, making almost a U-turn, onto a rough stony trail and through iron gates. (The large gates ahead of you only lead into the farm.) This rough trail descends to cross the Llores streambed, then starts to climb slightly upwards, rounding the cultivated area, and re-crossing the stream. Now our route begins to climb in earnest, up to the Coll de Biniamar. This is a fairly steep ascent, taking about three-quarters of an hour. This climb can be quite unpleasant on a hot day. At about **1h50min** you will reach the *coll* where, thankfully, the path levels out a bit and a breeze cools you.

Once on the heights, keep a sharp look-out for the path leading off down left to Sa Costera. You'll meet it in about five minutes' walking, just by a bend in the main track. A pile of rocks indicates the beginning of this narrow path,

Bálitx – the setting for Picnic 8 – is a wonderland of terracing and olive groves. This photograph was taken only five minutes beyond the Mirador de Ses Barques (see also photograph on page 27)

which starts by a type of gate entrance marked with red paint. Ignore the path on the right met in a few moments; it only rejoins the main Cala Tuent route. Continue down through the thickly pine-covered hillside towards the sea. It takes about half an hour to reach the cliffs at Sa Costera, where a large old house, mostly in ruins, overlooks the picturesque bay of Es Racó de Sa Taleca from its vantage point high up on the cliffs. Find the spring hiding in the dark stone tunnel, just up on a ridge behind the house, where you can cool your drinks in the icy water while you prepare your picnic lunch on the makeshift wooden table under the young olive tree. The blue waters of the bay below shimmer invitingly, and there is a (very steep) path down to the *cala*, but the energy required to venture down for a swim and then climb back up would far outweigh the pleasures of this excursion! Those making the Alternative walk will wend their way from here back to the Mirador de Ses Barques along the same route (under 5 hours).

Or, if you're lucky enough to be making the walk in the summer, let's carry on to Cala Tuent and La Calobra. You'll rejoin the main route in about **2h50min** walking. Turn left and wind your way on downhill, towards the ruins of an old electricity plant. You'll pass the small path leading down to it at about **3h15min** into the walk.

From here it's another hour and a quarter to the pretty little cove of Cala Tuent (**4h30min**). From Cala Tuent, follow the road up and over the hill in the direction of La Calobra. This final ascent is rather irksome, but you can take a short break at the top of the rise to visit the small thirteenth-century chapel of San Lorenzo, one of the oldest buildings on Mallorca, before you finally descend to La Calobra (**6h**).

9 EL TORRENTE DE PAREIS

See MAP on reverse of touring map; see also photograph page 55
Distance: 7km/4¼mi; 4h from Escorca (10.5km/6¼mi; 6h from Lluc)
Grade: Ⓖ; difficult; only recommended for expert walkers
Equipment: walking boots, extra socks and cardigans, torch, whistle, sunhat, picnic, water, anorak in cool weather
How to get there: 🚌 to Inca (for Lluc); but see STOP PRESS, p136
Train departs Palma 09.00; arrives Inca 09.35; bus waits outside station and departs 09.45 for Lluc; arrives Lluc 10.20
To return: ⛴ from La Calobra: see notes Walk 8, page 81
Short walk: explore the gorge from La Calobra — an easy outing.
Train to Sóller; tram to the port; boat to La Calobra: find convenient times in the schedules p132. Sunhat, swimwear, picnic, wading shoes

Following the course of the Torrente de Pareis is perhaps the most spectacular excursion on foot in Mallorca. But it's not for the inexperienced: you'll have to scramble over slippery rocks and boulders, wade through pools — and maybe even swim! — if you make the walk early in summer, after a wet spring. And this *is* a walk for summer months only — May to September.

With luck, you'll find a taxi driver at Lluc, waiting for a client and willing to take you to Escorca; more likely, you'll have to take the route that starts at the left of the monastery and climbs past the Finca Son Massip (see map). The *times given below* are based on departure from the Restaurante de Escorca, where **the walk** really **begins**.

Opposite the restaurant at Escorca, go through the gates to the old thirteenth-century church of Sant Pere. Just past the church, take the steps on the left, up to the old olive tree, and follow the path to the right. Come to two gates, and go through the brown rusty gate on the left. When you come to a large waste-disposal bin, turn sharp left. Now follow down, alongside the low stone wall on the left and at **10min** climb over the small iron gate. Continue down the rocky path and at **15min** *turn sharp*

From this fanciful rock arch you can look down into the Torrente de Pareis (Picnic 9b)

left at the olive tree with a black circle painted on it. Go down as far as the rocks, where you turn left again, and then right — red arrows now indicate the way, and the path also is easy to see from now on, as it winds on down towards the bed of the *torrente*. You can already see the gorge.

You'll reach the *voltes llargues* (the long bends) at **30min**, and in **1h** the path passes under the branches of a fig tree, where — some 20m (yds) or so further ahead, you must find the path off to the right, down through the rocks and long grasses. This is not easily seen, but starts more or less just as the main path begins to bend upwards again.

Five to ten minutes later should find you at the bottom, amongst the strewn rocks and boulders of the Torrente de Lluc. The scenery here is very impressive. Turn left down the Torrente de Lluc and find the grassy path on the left that will lead you first up above the rocks on the streambed and then down again into the wider Entreforc (**1h20min**). Here at the Entreforc, the Torrente de Lluc unites with the waters coming from Sa Fosca*, to form the Torrente de Pareis (the 'twin streams'). Down here, dwarfed by sheer rock faces and vertical cliffs, the walker is surrounded by a fantastic landscape. The strip of sky above seems far, far away, and the cry of wild birds and the hollow bleat of mountain goats echo mysteriously between the rock walls.

A large rock, more or less in the centre where the twin torrents converge, has a red cross painted across the top, showing Lluc to the south, La Calobra to the north, Sa Fosca (the 'dark place') off to the left, and — written in the Mallorcan dialect — 'Millor no enerí' (Better not go!), indicating the sheer rock wall on the right.

To begin down the Torrente de Pareis, follow over to the right from the red-painted rock, and find the small path that leads up through the long grass (there are one or two more red arrow guides). And, really, from here on, explanations are superfluous. It is simply a matter of finding the best way down the streambed, over the rocks and through the narrow passes. This is a very popular excursion amongst Mallorcans, so the best way to tackle the difficult spots is to seek out the well-worn, bottom-polished rocks. . . .

---

*Sa Fosca is a very exciting — and dangerous — place. Hardy and experienced rock climbers, in guided groups, and equipped with ropes and inflatable rafts, can explore these small underground lakes. The first two men to do this, both Mallorcan, were lost for forty-eight hours — unable to find their way out and unable to go back! If you decide to venture in a little way, be warned: *there are high, slippery boulders, and you will be literally 'in the dark' (fosca).*

10 A RAMBLE ROUND THE PUIG MAYOR*

Distance: 6 km/3¾mi; 2½h   **See MAP on reverse of touring map**
Grade: easy after initial climb

Equipment: stout shoes, sunhat, plastic bottle with water purifying tablets (water in summer), anorak and cardigans in winter

How to get there: hired car (or taxi hired from Sóller station) to K2.2 marker on the road to La Colobra; but see **STOP PRESS**, p136
To return: see 'Language hints', p63, if you wish to ask a taxi driver to return for you or to collect you on the C710

Short walk: as far as the oaks and return (A→B→A: 3km/1¾mi; 1h); equipment as above; easy after initial 15-20min climb

Alternative walk: via Coll d'es Carscolers to C710 (A→B→C→D: 5.5km/3¼mi; 2¼h); transport required on C710 near K38 stone

The deposits of a lagoon where, millions of years ago, prehistoric species abounded in the waters and swamps of the Eocene period, can still be found along a five- or six-kilometre band on the northern slopes of the Puig Mayor. This area, at a height of some 700—900m, runs from Es Clot near Fornalutx as far as the fountain of Sa Baume, which we pass by in this walk. Originally the band was much longer and wider, but the violence with which the mountains thrust themselves upwards forced the strata up to their present height. The hard white rocks break off easily into thin slates of stone when hit, and these strata contain some of the richest fossil flora known on Mallorca. This walk along the northern slopes of the island's highest mountain gives us not only the chance to see some of these beautiful and interesting white rock formations, but also lets us admire the picturesque little valley of Bini, with its stream trickling down towards the cliffs, as well as some spectacular views of the coastline and the Puig Mayor dominating the landscape at 1445m/4740ft.

Begin the walk at K2.2 on the road to La Colobra (there is plenty of room to leave a car). There's a large stone platform here. From the stone wall, facing Puig Mayor, bear up slightly to the right, where you will find a wide track. Cross this, and continue straight up ahead, where, a minute later, the narrow rocky path begins by the side of a young wild olive tree and a rock splashed with red paint. Start climbing up the slope, heading for the electricity pylons, and later following alongside an old water channel. By about **15min** you'll have passed an old sheep fold and found a gap in the stone wall. Walk through, and you're on the northern slopes of the Puig Mayor, where the way levels out. From here there are excellent views of the coast near La Calobra and an old *atalaya* on the hilltop across the valley.

*The summit bears a military installation and is inaccessible

Pass a small spring at **25min** (dry in summer) and in **30min** go through a gate in a stone wall. Down right are the stone foundations of an old farm. From here an old stone trail leads towards Bini valley. A few minutes along from the gate, you can see the steep slopes of the mighty Puig Mayor towering majestically above you to the left. There are not many trees in this area, which is characterised by bare and jagged rocks alternating with wind-blown long golden grass, forming a series of lonely hills and valleys that reach down to the coastline. However, you will pass by a small group of oaks standing bravely on the bare slope at about **35min**.

Continuing along, the way is now an old moss-covered trail, lined with bracken. Meet more gates at **50min**: just past here is the wide earth track between the C710 and the Bini farms. (For the Alternative walk, follow the track up left; it will take you through lovely oak woods on the Coll d'es Carscolers ridge, to the C710 (900m below the tunnel). Be sure to have transport waiting! (see **STOP PRESS**, p136).

Our continuing (right-hand) track leads down into the valley of Bini. Walking along here, some five minutes later, you will be able to look down into this beautiful valley, unbelievably green in winter and early spring, contrasting with the bareness of the surrounding mountains. The houses of Bini Petit and Bini Grand lie sheltered and protected from the raw sea winds of winter, whilst their sheep graze undisturbed on these rich green pastures.

We can walk as far as the farmhouses, going through the gate (1h into the walk), and turning left through the second gate just before the buildings, continuing on to the stream. A quaint little bridge crosses the stream here, and then the way continues up the rocky slope to where the house of Bini Grand hides in the trees. Now that the Montcaire lands are closed to walkers (see also Walk 8), we must either re-trace our steps or go to the C710 via the Carscolers Pass.

A few oaks on the bare slopes of the Puig Mayor (Picnic 10)

11 CANALETAS OLD AND NEW: CUBER · GORG BLAU · ES PRAT · LA CANALETA DE MASSANELLA · TOSSALS · CUBER

Distance: 11km/6¾mi; 4½h   **See MAP on reverse of touring map**

Grade: fairly easy: level walking along new aqueduct path, followed by gentle ups and downs (on generally rocky paths)

Equipment: stout walking shoes or boots, sunhat, picnic, plastic bottle with water purifying tablets, anorak in winter

How to get there: hired car to the Cúber reservoir (or taxi from Soller or Inca); but see also **STOP PRESS**, page 136
To return: See 'Language hints', page 63, if you wish to ask a taxi driver to wait for you at the Cúber Reservoir, or to return for you

Short walk: Cúber Reservoir to Canaleta de Massanella and return (A→B→A: 7.5km/4½mi; 2¾h); grade and equipment as above

The faint tinkling of sheep bells in the distance, the wind whispering its secrets in the valley, and the restful flow of moving waters are the only sounds that penetrate the impressive silence of the mountains in this beautiful part of the *sierra*. And even these sounds disappear once you've reached the mountainside of Tossals Verts, where the silence is almost as wonderful as the majesty of the peaks.

Start the walk at the Cúber reservoir on the C710. Walk east on the main road for a few minutes, to find the crossing of the modern aqueduct. Some 30m (yds) further along, a track leads up right to a path beside this *canaleta* (you can join *at* the aqueduct crossing, but there's a marshy spot here which the track avoids). At first you'll meet a couple of wet patches on the path; but there are detours round them, or else you can cross on large stones.

Following along, hopefully beside rushing waters, you'll find that this level, easy path quickly rises well above the C710 and in **10min** you'll have a superb overview of the Gorg Blau reservoir. Several good promontories overlook it,

Picnic 11 overlooks the Gorg Blau from a pine-shaded knoll

but the best one for picnicking is reached in half an hour, on a rocky outcropping shaded by evergreen oaks.

This modern *canaleta* takes water piped up from the Gorg Blau (you can see the pipe at the western end of that reservoir) and carries it to the Cuber, from where it is piped to Palma.

Having passed a couple of small 'flyovers' on the channel, in **45min** walking you'll come to a proper bridge over the aqueduct. Cross it, and start up a wide and rocky path. Soon meet a stone wall, where you can pass through a gap (but if it has been repaired, there's a hand-made ladder to help you over). Just beyond the wall, to the left, is a trig point. We soon approach a pass, the Coll d'es Coloms. At 822m, this is the highest point of the walk. From here the Puig de Massanella (Walk 12) rises in the east some 500m/1650ft above us.

At **1h10min** the old farmhouse of Es Prat comes into view, half hidden amongst the trees, Climb the gate and pass by the abandoned corral. The main path continues ahead, but be sure to fork up left by the first *sitja* on a smaller path. This leads to the front of the Es Prat house, from where you have a splendid view of the distant mountain of Randa on the far horizon, across the plain between other mountains — an original and picturesque backcloth for a photograph.

Continuing on past the house, rejoin the main path and at **1h20min** you will find the Font d'es Prat de Massanella, the spring which feeds the Canaleta de Massanella. A large, open clearing, with plenty of shade from the ubiquitous evergreen oaks, invites us to lay down our rucksacks and drink plentifully from the crystal-clear, sparkling waters that flow from this ancient well. Right down inside the well, the date 1748 is engraved in the stonework, the year in which the construction of this old *canaleta* was begun.*

Before you leave Es Prat, you may like to explore a bit on the old pilgrims' trail to Lluc (see footnote page 77). Now completely lost north of Massanella, it once passed by here.

---

*The history of the *canaleta* is interesting. The work is attributed to a Montserrat Fontanet, a Mallorcan pig farmer employed on the Massanella farmholding during the 18th century. The owner of this large property had brought engineers from France, England, Italy and the Spanish mainland, to plan and execute the channelling of water from the Prat spring. All these eminent engineers agreed that the feat was technically impossible, after which Señor Fontanet offered to do the job himself. His employer agreed to his suggestion, and the work was reportedly completed in two years — a record feat by any standards!

Now double back on your tracks, to visit the *canaleta* itself. About 60m (yds) back from the spring, you'll see a three-pronged fork in the main route: at your left, a path crosses a stream; the main path goes straight ahead. We take the way that runs at a 45-degree angle between these two. The stream will be on our left as we follow this middle path. The old Canaleta de Massanella is hidden beneath our feet, but the stonework emerges to the surface some 300m (yds) further along — by some lovely pools. This is a superb place for picnicking, beside the running (overspill) waters, in the shade of oaks. The only disappointment is that the *canaleta* is no longer free-flowing. There was a great outcry from local conservationists when the waters of this national monument were encased in piping in 1983.

It used to be a wonderful adventure to follow the *canaleta* from here: one climbed the high stone wall of Es Molinot (the old mill, the remains of which may still be seen down in the valley) and had to proceed very carefully along a very narrow stretch for about five minutes, as the channel rounded the side of the mountain. If you're not subject to vertigo, and you're sure-footed, about five minutes along from the Es Molinot wall, you will be able to see the arched aqueduct that carries the *canaleta* across a ravine — still a beautiful sight. The channel continues from there, through waterfalls and tunnels, into the village of Mancor del Valle, about six kilometres southeast.

Now let's make for the old farm at Tossals Verts, where we can picnic on a grassy slope, surrounded by high mountains on all sides. If you've ventured along the water channel, turn back, climb over the wall, and make a descent into the valley of S'Avenc d'en Ferré, following alongside the old stone wall, crossing the Es Prat stream, and making your way up the opposite mountainside, where you'll find the path that rounds Tossals Verts.

Head south, and a large boulder appears below in the valley, called Es Castellot. (Beyond it, and to the right, one can explore the caves in the hillside. But beware: the descent is difficult, and there is no path.) The views from our mountainside route are very good: the village of Selva lies peacefully across the Massanella valley, and the Puig de Inca and the mountains of Artá far to the east can be seen. Soon (2h30min) see the old stone wall of the *finca* of Tossals Verts, a long-abandoned farm. Passing through a gap in the wall, you will soon find a wide grassy area on the open mountainside, by an old well — the Font de Sa Basola — another ideal spot for lunch.

12 LLUC · PUIG DE MASSANELLA · LLUC

See MAP on reverse of touring map; see photograph page 99
Distance: 12km/7¼mi; 5h
Grade: Ⓖ ; strenuous; danger of thick mists and vertigo
Equipment: walking boots, long trousers, cardigans, sunhat, anorak, whistle, torch, picnic, plastic bottle with water purifying tablets
How to get there: 🚌 to Inca
Depart Palma 09.00; arriva Inca 09.35, to connect with 🚌 to Lluc, which waits outside station and departs 09.45; arrives Lluc 10.20
NB: for *this* walk, do not go into Lluc, but ask to be put off at the petrol station before Lluc ('estación de servicio de Lluc, por favor')
To return: 🚌 from Lluc (or petrol station) to Inca: departs Lluc 18.00; arrives Inca 18.30. 🚌 departs Inca 19.00; arrives Palma 19.35
NB: See STOP PRESS, p136, if you're staying in Sóller or Pollensa
Short walk: as far as you like along the path of the main walk, perhaps as far as the first indication stones (A→B→A: 5km/3mi; 1¾h *return*); equipment as above (except torch); no guide necessary

T he Puig de Massanella is that double-peaked, high rock mountain, in the northern stretch of the *sierra*, visible from many parts of the island. The second highest peak on Mallorca, it reaches up 1352m (4435ft). And about 150m below the summit, the freshwater spring of the Font de S'Avenc, hidden deep in the mountainside, bubbles fresh, cool, filtered water almost all the year round.

The walk begins at the petrol station south of Lluc. About 150m (yds) below the station, find green gates on your right; a block of stone to the left is engraved 'Puig de Massanella'. Go through the gates and take the first turning right (a short cut). Right again, 20m or so up, by a rock with a red paint daub. You will soon rejoin the main route, where you'll see a large, red paint-marked rock. From here, take the narrow path up to the right (a continuation of the short cut), again rejoining the main track. Now along the main route, you will meet a gate at 15min. Climb over a stile at the right. Soon you'll see the farm buildings of Comafreda on your right, in open fields across the stream.

At 25min, on approaching the old gate in the stone wall, turn up to the left just before the gate, following the marks on the wall itself. The way to the right leads to the farmhouse, and the trail straight ahead through the gates is the old pilgrims' route between Lluc and Sóller (see Walks 7 and 11), unfortunately now impassable around Massanella.

Our rocky path up left heads through oaks, marked with red paint. At 30min, go over the remains of an old stone wall, almost in ruins, and a minute later, continue straight on (another short cut). Climb up ancient stony steps, turning left where the paint splashes indicate. Rejoin the main way in five minutes, and turn up left, following red arrows.

At **40min** turn right, still following the main route, and on arriving at a small clearing (just by an old stone *refugio*), turn up the rocky slope towards the left, where you will see a large red arrow on the rock, pointing upwards. Red paint marks now guide us up through the Pas de N'Arbona.

Ten minutes later, you will come to another clearing. On the left, there is the Puig de N'Alí (1038m), before we come to the two large indication stones. 'Puig de Massanella', clearly engraved on one of them, indicates a sharp turn to the right from here, following the red arrows up through the trees, and bearing right. Now the path begins to wind up rather more steeply. From here onwards, keep a sharp lookout for the red paint marks, as the path can be difficult to distinguish from time to time, until we reach the summit in about another 90 minutes.

At **1h**, you'll see a large red II painted on the rock, on a bend in the path. Further on up, the view begins to attract our attention, and it is advisable to stop for a breather from time to time, to admire the splendid scenery. The plain stretches out below, down to the southern coastline and the city of Palma, where the wide bay shimmers in the sun and a misty haze hides the horizon.

Passing between large boulders, trees and long grasses, our path has become very rocky indeed. Always keep a keen lookout for the red paint marks! At **1h25min** at the Avenc del Camí, a mountain 'crossroads', there is a small hole down to a cave on the right of the path. Careful, it's very deep! Now find the indication stone, which directs two ways: to the Font de S'Avenc straight on, and to the summit, up the rocky slope. It you wish to go straight to the peak, the path is quite easily seen from here; but coming down to the fountain, it is difficult to see the red marks on the steep descent. So let's make the tour in a clockwise direction, first visiting the fountain and taking a breather. When we reach the summit, our return path will be easy to find.

Our path to the fountain climbs two stony slopes, the way indicated by red paint and small piles of rocks, generally bearing left. At **1h35min**, come to a wide open rock slope and head up right towards the large and solitary oak. Past here, a long stretch of treeless jagged rocks and boulders is seen ahead, before the red paint marks take us to the Font de S'Avenc (**1h45min**). This is a marvellous place. Stone steps lead down into the mountain, like the entrance to an Aladdin's Cave. You'll need a torch — it's pitch black!

An indication stone at the fountain shows the way up, and there's a good deal of clambering over high rocks. One feels infinitely minute, nothing but a speck of humanity, slowly crawling up this massive rocky mountain, like a tiny ant labouring over a boulder.

In **2h30min** you will reach the top! And the panorama is of course worth every minute of the effort. The whole of the island lies below you, a magical landscape of mountains, hills and valleys, surrounded by the blue Mediterranean. You're on the highest accessible peak on Mallorca, now that the Puig Mayor is closed because of the radar station. In your wonder and admiration, don't forget to be careful — just below the peak is one of the island's deepest snow pits!

Looking down towards the left, facing the plain, you will be able to see a tiny path way below on a sort of flat tableland area at the foot of the rocky slope. We'll make for this route, as we begin the descent. It's really fairly easy, jumping from rock to boulder, boulder to rock, and takes about twenty minutes to reach the path. And from here back, the way is very easy to follow, right to the Lluc road.

The well-kept woodlands of ICONA, on the Binifaldó road (Picnic 14)

13 AROUND THE PUIG ROIG: LLUC · MOSSA · COLL D'ELS ASES · COSCONAS · LLUC

Distance: 19km/11½mi; 7h **See MAP on reverse of touring map**

Grade: moderate, over well-defined, but sometimes very stony paths; some **danger of vertigo** by Coll d'els Ases and beyond

Equipment: stout shoes or boots, anorak, sunhat, picnic, plastic bottle with water purifying tablets, cardigan

How to get there: see Walk 12 (for Lluc); see also **STOP PRESS**, p136

Short walk: Lluc to Ca'n Pontico and return (**A→B→A:** 8km/5mi; 2¾h); easy; take stout shoes, picnic, water, sunhat. Follow the lane to the left of the monastery (between it and the bar-café)

Alternative walks: Lluc to Cosconás and return (**A→C→A:** 13km/7¾mi; 5h) or Mossa to Cosconás as main walk, returning to Mossa by a path on the south side of Puig Roig (**D→C→D:** 12km/7½mi; 5h)

The long and winding path that rounds the Puig Roig (the Red Mountain) offers some magnificent panoramas along the wild and rugged coastline near La Calobra, and by far the island's best views of the Puig Mayor. Although this is a very long walk, it is certainly not difficult, and anyone stoutly shod with plenty of stamina can do it.

Start out from Lluc as in Walk 14 (see page 98), to join the C710 in **25min.** Follow the road to Mossa's gates (**1h**). (See also **STOP PRESS**, page 136: you may be able to get a bus from Lluc to Mossa, saving one hour.) Go in the Mossa gates, and follow the earth track (ignoring a path to the left). Continuing on towards the right, some 50m (yds) further along, you will pass through another gate. Looking to the left, the red cliffsides of the long and high Puig Roig now dominate the landscape. Passing through another gate in ten minutes, the still air is full of the delightful tinkling of countless sheepbells, as you approach Mossa's farm.

The track now leads slightly upwards, rounding the farm and passing another gateway. Walk quietly here, being as unprovocative as possible to the loudly-barking farm dogs. Don't worry — they are usually all chained up and won't bother to keep up this cacophony once you have gone through the gates to the left of the old house.

Now continue straight ahead, crossing a small patch of rocky terrain, where you will find the narrow, rocky path directly in front of you. Pass through the gap in an old stone wall and soon you will have some splendid views of the pretty little Mossa river valley gradually falling away below. As you come up to the pass, the Coll d'els Ases, the last lap rounds a steep cliffside — with some danger of vertigo. You'll reach the *coll* at 1h50min, and soon catch your first glimpse of the sea. The panorama from this saddle at 627m/2055ft is wonderful. Behind, to the southeast, the Puig Tomir (Walk 14) thrusts its wide, triangular-shaped peak into the sky. On your left, the Sierra de la Mola del Teix — at its most beautiful when covered with snow — edges the landscape with majesty.

On the right, almost treeless mountains undulate down to an indigo sea. Just behind these mountains is the *come-*

dero, the vultures' feeding ground. Because of the lack of suitable food for this endangered species, ICONA takes a weekly supply of carrion, thus ensuring the survival of these beautiful birds. There are few left, but this is one of the areas where you are most likely to spot their enormous, dark silhouettes, with the characteristic pointed tail.

The rocky and exciting path continues now for over two hours more, rounding the whole of the north side of the Puig Roig, with magnificent views over the abutment, the Morro de Sa Vaca, jutting out just before the bay of La Calobra, and the Morro d'els Bordils, where the ancient

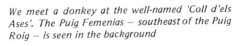

We meet a donkey at the well-named 'Coll d'els Ases'. The Puig Femenias — southeast of the Puig Roig — is seen in the background

watchtower of Lluc has looked out over the sea for centuries. (There used to be a path to this *atalaya*, but the way
is no longer safe.) Further along, we have the island's most
dramatic view of its highest peak, the mighty Puig Mayor.

Pass between some huge solitary pines growing on the
bare mountainside, and in five minutes you will arrive at a
long, low stone wall which runs down the hillside as far
as the old house of the *carabineros*. To reach this old civil
guards' house, you'll have to clamber down the hillside
beside the wall — it takes about fifteen minutes. The civil
guard, although supposedly here to guard the coast, spent
most of their time trading illegally with smugglers. By night
local workers carried great sacks of tobacco, coffee and
sugar smuggled ashore from Africa, along this very same
path to the north of the Red Mountain — it's the old
smugglers' route that we've been following from Mossa.

Having explored for a while, take the path that leads
away through the gate just down in front of the house.
Continue along here for about five minutes, and you will
come to an enclosure, as the path makes a U-turn. Climb
up a few metres on the farther side and, just behind a
corrugated roof covering a water tank, you'll find a spring
(best to use water purifying tablets here) coming out of a
small tunnel in the hillside. Slightly up to the right of this
you will find a flat grassy patch shaded by a group of pines,
the perfect spot for a picnic and a rest, enjoying the magnificent views of Puig Mayor and the high *sierra*.

The return journey begins on the same route, at the
foot of the spring, turning left after descending from the
picnic area, and following along a wide but rocky path.
Take no notice of the red arrow on a rock pointing uphill
ten minutes further along (unless you are making the alternative walk and wish to visit the civil guards' house — this is
only a shortcut to it). Pass through two sets of gates to see
the pretty olive-covered slopes going down into the Lluc
stream valley. Further down, you'll see the *entreforc*, where
the waters from the Torrente de Lluc and Sa Fosca unite to
form the Torrente de Pareis (our Walk 9).

At about **4h45min**, passing through more gates, you will
see the amazing old houses of Cosconás, built into the
natural caves in the mountainside. From Cosconás back to
Lluc the track is flat and wide — very comfortable for
walking. It winds on down the south side of the Puig Roig,
through farmlands, apple orchards, almond trees and some
terraces populated by thousand-year-old olive trees, twisted
by age into highly imaginative forms.

Sóller

(Note that you can also return from Cosconás to Mossa, by rounding the south side of the Puig Roig. This route is about 12km; there's a good path starting just past Cosconás.)

The main walk keeps to the track, passing by the gates of the *finca* of Sa Plana on the left, and soon after, an old abandoned house with a sun dial on its walls. Neat stone walls and wrought iron gates, through which many well-kept gardens may be glimpsed, mark your approach to Ca'n Pontico. Cross a small bridge over the (generally dry) Mossa stream and then stride out through flat open fields before you start to wind your way up to Lluc, where a large cross is visible at the top of the hill. Making a final effort on these last tiring uphill bends, you soon reach a tarmac road — a continuation of the track. It leads right into the monastery forecourt and the oasis of a bar-café (7h).

The Puig Mayor is glimpsed through the pass at Alaró; the bluffs of El Puig de Alaró (left) and S'Alcanada (right) frame the photograph

14 A SCRAMBLE UP THE PUIG TOMIR

See map on reverse of the touring map; see photograph page 93
Distance: 12km/7¼mi; 5h

Grade: strenuous, with possibility of thick mists and vertigo. Two scree areas to be crossed. For experienced mountain walkers only

Equipment: walking boots, long trousers, sunhat, whistle, picnic, water, walking stick; cardigans, anorak and headgear in cool weather

How to get there: see Walk 12 (for Lluc); see also **STOP PRESS**, p136

Short walk: Lluc to Finca Binifaldó and return (A→B→A: 5km/3mi; under 2h). Easy. Take sunhat, picnic, water and enjoy a woodland stroll; picnic spots abound, especially on the Binifaldó road

More a mountaineering adventure than a walk, this scramble is only for the sure-footed. But anyone can enjoy the pleasant woodland stroll during the first hour, by following the tarmac lane to the foot of Tomir.

If the weather is dry, but not too hot, and you're really fit, off we go. The fantastic views from Tomir's peak (1107m/3630ft) — the third highest on the island — make the effort well worth while. A magnificent panorama of hills, mountains, plains, wide bays and coastline will unfold itself before your eyes — an eagle's eye view of Mallorca!

To start out, leave Lluc by the main gates. About 100m (yds) along the secondary road, come to an entrance on the left. Turn in, and take the path to the right, through the football pitch and past the *fronton* courts. Now the way is a picturesque old track, winding gracefully through trees and rocks eroded into wonderfully whimsical shapes. We pass by a picnic and camping area, and at **25min** come out on the main C710. Turn left here, and walk for about 100m (yds) to the K17.4 stone. Here, on the right, are the gates to Binifaldó and a large wooden ICONA sign.

Turn into the lane (the old route to Pollensa) leading to ICONA's headquarters, and enjoy the gentle uphill stroll through well-kept woodlands and ever more wonderfully-formed rocks (see the photograph on page 93; this is a lovely picnic area). In **35min** you'll meet some sets of green gates. Opt for the left-hand gate, and continue along the old Lluc—Pollensa road until a group of poplars announces your arrival at the *finca* of Binifaldó (**55min**). The old road continues on through the gates over left, just beyond the poplars. Today's walk lies straight ahead, however: in **1h 15min** you'll come to tall iron gates at the entrance to the water-bottling plant at the Binifaldó fountain.

The path up Tomir begins on the right, on the other side of the boundary fence, just by the gates. Follow alongside the fence, and in about five minutes keep a very sharp eye out for the red arrow on the rock at ground level, pointing up to the right. It is easily missed, because the path along-side the fence continues ahead. We turn right, following a path winding up the mountainside. A minute later, another arrow points left, where the path bends sharply, and then turns up to the right again.

Soon you'll come to the first scree area — said to be the remains of a glacier. Go carefully, and only *after* you have safely crossed should you stop to admire the surrounding landscapes, the setting for so many other walks: Lluc's valley, the double-peaked Puig de Massanella, Puig Roig and Puig Mayor. It all leaves you breathless — apart from the climb! Now we hike up the steep side of the cliff, up to a small pass. From here, Palma is visible on the south coast, and a rest is advisable, not only to admire the views, but also to catch your breath before starting to cross the second scree. *Extra care is needed here, and do not attempt to cross the scree in dangerous conditions — just after snow or rain, for example. There are many loose stones and rocks.*

At about **1h55min**, you will have to clamber over the rock face, after which the path is rather camouflaged as it crosses the rocky terrain. Head east, following the rocky way, and keeping the two peaks on your left — bearing right where, from time to time, you can see the red arrows on the rocks. At about **2h5min** go left by a pile of rocks, and continue on upwards, keeping left, following the arrows up to the second, higher peak. You should arrive here at about **2h15min** into the walk.

The view is really fantastic, but there is more to come! Keep on, bearing left, for what seems an endless clamber over rocks and low rosemary-scented scrub, towards the highest part of the *puig* until you reach the true, 1107m-high summit, at **2h45min**. (Beneath the iron cross is a very deep snow pit.) Now you have the world at your feet. Perhaps this is the best vantage point on the island from which to appreciate the beauty of the bays and headlands in the northeast, the landscapes of Walks 17-25.

A typical 'sitja'; this one is on the Puig de Massanella (Picnic 12)

15 CAMPANET · BINIATRO · SES FONS · AUCANELLA · BINIBONA · CAIMARI

Distance: 16km/9¾mi; under 6h

Grade: moderate, with a gentle, steady uphill climb

Equipment: stout shoes (boots in winter), whistle, insect repellant, long-sleeved shirt and long trousers (see notes in text), cardigan and long anorak, as well as waterproof trousers in winter, picnic, water

How to get there: 🚍 to Inca
Departs Palma 09.00; arrives Inca 09.35
Taxi from Inca station: ask for 'Cuevas de Campanet'
NB: on Sundays *only*, there is a bus direct to Campanet at 09.00, but the walk from Campanet to the Oratorio will take about 1 hour
To return: 🚍 from Caimari to Inca. This is the Lluc bus; last departure from Lluc 18.00; passes Caimari 18.15; arrives Inca 18.30
🚍 from Inca to Palma: departs 19.00; arrives 19.35

Short/Alternative walks: use the map to explore as you like from either Campanet or Caimari, making easy walks (stout shoes, sun-hat, picnic, water). There's a bus to Campanet at 12.45, and at 09.00 *Sundays only*, with convenient return times (see Timetable p130). The Lluc bus passes Caimari, and the convenient Selva buses bring you to the PM213 just 2km below Caimari. See Timetables p130-32. From Campanet (**A**), visit the Oratorio (**B**) and the caves or the Font d'els Cipresos (**C**); from Caimari (**D**) visit Binibona (**E**)

A beautiful walk, the Campanet—Caimari route begins in the attractive woodland area of the foothills just below the Puig Tomir (Walk 14). Tall and dominant ever-green oaks, the occasional eucalyptus, and delicately-perfumed *Erica multiflora* grow in quiescent harmony on the sloping hillsides, serenaded by the song of the nightingale in spring, and dappled by shafts of golden sunlight. Pine

forests further up suddenly open out into a wide *pla*, or tableland, surrounded on all sides by the mountains, and the route descends later through dense under-growth and thick forest to the pretty smallholding of Binibona, from where a narrow country lane ribbons its way over low hills to the mountain village of Cai-mari. Although the walk is fairly long, it's not too taxing — especially on a coolish day — and the beauty and stillness of the woodlands and artistically-landscaped hillsides are ample compensation.

Start the walk on the old Campanet—Pollensa road, in front of the Oratorio of San Miguel (see page 105), a pretty 13th-century church just south of the Cuevas de Campanet. Continue straight ahead on

In the foothills of the Puig Tomir (2h30min)

this road, keeping left at a fork. Soon you'll see the large old house of Biniatró up ahead on the hillside. You'll pass two old cypress trees and a small ruin on your right, before you spot the track up to Biniatró (**30min**), which begins almost opposite the ruins of an old *casita*.

This old track leads up between two low stone walls. It crosses the *torrente* and then goes over open fields, climbing gradually up into the foothills. Soon you will arrive at the enormous old farmstead of Biniatró (**45min**), once the home of the several families needed to tend the lands and harvest the crops of this extensive *finca*. If you are lucky enough to find the shutters open on the third window along from the door, you will be able to see the enormous wooden screws on the ancient olive-press that produced oil in this once-thriving community.

The way continues through the beautiful farmlands, past the gardens on the right (now sadly abandoned) and a multitude of olive trees up on the rocky slopes. Then you'll pass through the iron gate to the Ses Fons holding. Here you will see a sign, 'Prohibido el Paso'. You *do* have the right of way — to the Font d'els Cipresos — but should you meet anyone here, it would be best to ask permission to pass through the *finca* (see page 63, 'Meeting a landowner'). Cypress trees grow alongside the stream in the valley on the left, and the surrounding fields, emerald-green even in the winter, provide pasture for grazing sheep. Ignore a small path bending down to the left just by an iron gate. Five minutes later, go through the gates ahead of you, and take the track immediately to the left (through another gate), crossing the stream bed. Then bear right past an old oak, towards a *sitja*. The track is easily visible from here: it leads into the woods. Through the trees, you will soon be able to see the big house of Ses Fons on the hillside over right. Keeping to the main route, and ignoring various *caminos forrestales* branching off, you'll pass by an old well at the side of a long-disused *sitja*. Here, the delicate perfume of the *Erica multiflora* wafts on the breeze, and you'll recognise the odd strawberry tree and mastic bushes. The bell-like song of the nightingale echoes clearly through the tall oaks, and the mating call of the Hoopoe rings out incessantly — all tell-tale signs of Nature's most magnificent adventure, spring — if you make the walk at the right time of the year.

As we continue uphill, high rocky mountains soon appear on our right. Ignoring all offshoots of our moss-edged trail, we pass through a gate, with the stream still on our right. Then we leave the stream to climb the wooded slopes in a series of bends, until we reach a small clearing on the left.

Soon the oaks give way to pines and thicker undergrowth, and then we can see the distant bay of Alcudia and the marshlands of the Albufera lying on the horizon behind us to the right. Up ahead, the high and bare rocks of the Puig Tomir seem very close. A few minutes later (**2h**) we come to the Font d'els Cipresos, named for the abundant cypresses growing round the well. At the spring, the continuing right-hand path only leads up to the olive slopes; we take the path up left, which winds through pines and ferns towards the *pla*. (Be careful not to take the small path leading off right a bit further up; it only returns to the well.) Go through an old wooden gate, and continue straight ahead, across the open fields of the *planicie*. This wide, high, open space is wonderful after the long climb through the woods; breathe in the clear cool mountain air and admire your breathtakingly beautiful surroundings.

The old abandoned house of Aucanalleta lies ahead. Cross the broken stone wall and head towards the house (there's no track here). You may like to picnic at the house (**2h30min**), overlooking the pretty valley. From here there's no easily-discerned path for the next stretch of the walk, so follow the notes carefully! The second house of Aucanella is our next landmark. From the front of the house at Aucanalleta, take the *right-hand* opening in the stone wall of the patio, and follow down left, going down a rough path. Go through a small gate at the bottom (ignoring the 'Coto privado de caza' sign — this only means 'private hunting ground'). Continue over the rocks, straight ahead downhill, following the narrow path down to the open fields just below the house of Aucanella.

Our route does not visit the Aucanella house, but stays in the open fields well below it, bearing slightly left and making for a gap in the stone wall seen up ahead. Pass through the opening in the stone wall, and bear left across the wide open field, with the low stone wall running alongside on the left. Keep the pine-clad slope on your left, and the valley to the right. Head for the lowest part of the horizon, where you will come to a wire fence. There is a good picnic spot here, just to the left, where trees provide shade and the wall a back-rest.

Now begin the descent into the valley, by going through the large hole in the wire fence (4m/yds left of the tree), and turning left along the rocky path. Careful not to miss it! It's fairly camouflaged amongst the rocks. This narrow path leads you on down, through the thick undergrowth, between large rocks and boulders — the valley is still on your right. (This might be a good time to put on the long-sleeved shirt and long trousers you brought.)

On arriving at some large oak trees, the way continues ahead on a narrow path. A wire fence is close by at the right, and you can spot a house down right, across the stream bed. At a second group of oaks, the path heads down and slightly right amongst the rocks. Continuing on ahead and slightly downwards, you should be able to follow this overgrown path, quite narrow, but later widening out, through the trees.

Keeping to the ever-descending path, in a few minutes you'll pass the way across the stream to the house you glimpsed earlier on (3h40min). Keep on ahead, to go through the dilapidated old gate of the abandoned farm. From here, the path leads on through dense undergrowth, and if you have not yet put on long trousers and a long-sleeved shirt, this is the time to do so — especially in late spring or warmer weather. Watch out for horrible little *garrapatas* — ticks — which would love to get a chance to attach themselves to you. They can only be got rid of by burning them out with a cigarette end, or a visit to the doctor. They have a special predilection for the scalp.

But soon this stretch is behind us, and a beautiful, deep and rugged valley opens up on our right, as the stony path starts to climb upwards. We go through another gate, and the way flattens out and leads through a small pass. Beyond here, there's a magnificent view of the plain. An enormous boulder planted in the foreground makes this a good place for a bit of photography. Standing beside this huge rock, you can see the deep valley, thick with pines, below.

The Oratorio de San Miguel is just south of the entrance to the famous Cuevas de Campanet. If you enjoy an easy countryside stroll, take advantage of the good transport to Campanet and walk from there to this chapel (Picnic 15), perhaps going on to visit the caves.

Continuing the descent, we arrive at a large open clearing and take the path to the right through the woods. Ten minutes later, the path runs right into a *torrente*, but turn down along the stream bed, towards the left (plenty of stepping stones if there is water), for about 100m (yds), where the path re-emerges on the right. The way is now much better walking, by the high, pine-wooded cliff and the stream on the left. Ignore the small *camino forrestal* across the stream on your left; a couple of minutes later, we come to a large green gate: go through, but if you find it locked, you will have to climb the low stone wall and fence to the left. The way now crosses an open area, with the woods receding away to the right.

Follow the well-worn, red earth track until you come to a second green gate. Past here, turn left down a lane — which is soon tarmac-surfaced — and you'll soon come to Binibona (**5h20min**), where old farm buildings and elegant modern houses mingle together, oblivious of class distinctions. The lane then takes a turn to the right and becomes a tarmac country road. Continue straight ahead here (the small country lane leading down to the left goes to the village of Moscari).

This narrow road, bordered by wild asparagus bushes, and surrounded by rolling countryside, winds its way lazily over hills for another twenty-five minutes. You'll arrive at Caimari in about **6h** walking at most. Once into the village, make your way down the narrow streets, past the village square, towards the main road. Here you can stop the Lluc—Inca bus anywhere, as it passes through the village.

16 MORTITX · RAFAL DE ARIANT · SA COVA DE SES BRUIXES OVERLOOK · MORTITX

Distance: from Mortitx to Sa Cova de Ses Bruixes and return: 8km/4¾mi; 4h; to return via El Torrente de Mortitx add 1½km (1h)

Grade: very rocky, wild terrain makes the going a bit tricky, and the path is often difficult to distinguish. Only experts, with a guide, should attempt to return via the *torrente* and only in very dry conditions: some strenuous clambering over slippery rocks is involved

Equipment: walking boots, whistle, long trousers, water, picnic, cardigans and anorak with hood in winter; sunhat in hot weather

How to get there: 🚌 to Pollensa and return (all details page 130) *Taxi from Pollensa to Mortitx and return* (taxi rank is by bus stop); ask the driver to return for you — see 'Language hints', page 63, no later than 30 minutes before the return bus
NB: see also **STOP PRESS**, page 136

Short walk: as far as you like along the course of the main walk; the 'wild west' setting of fantastic rock formations surrounds you almost from the start; stout shoes will suffice for a short walk

---

The Rafal de Ariant Trail is an ancient, narrow, rocky path over some of the most wild and fantastic, rugged mountain terrain on Mallorca. The scenery along here is almost phantasmagoric — the shapes and strange formations of huge boulders and wind-sculptured rocks, strewn over the uneven surface of the mountains creating a wild and savage panorama. And an eerie silence, broken only by the wind and the occasional cry of some wild bird, lends an aura of mysticism to this unspoilt and uncivilised part of the *sierra*. Finally, the sheer coastal cliffs are reached, with drops of 200m/650ft straight down into the sea. Here the steep escarpment is riddled with fantastic huge caves carved out of the rock faces by the elements, and the sea foams white and savage on the rocks below.

It's a walk with a difference! And all the more exciting on a windy, winter's day, when the clouds cast their moving shadows over the mountains, so accentuating the shapes and shadows of the rocks. If you go in warm weather, a

Picnic 16: Mortitx. Notice the palm bush in the foreground

sunhat is a must — there is very little shade, except at the old abandoned houses of Rafal de Ariant.

Leave the taxi at the Mortitx gates (if you come by car, these lie between the 10 and 11 km markers on the C710; park well against the wall). **Start out** by passing two sets of gates and walking *past* the tennis court. Then go right through another gate at the left of a stone shed, and walk between two cherry plantations up to another gate on the left (**10min**). Just beyond this gate is a small grassy area with a fig tree. Then the path leads slightly upwards, by large rocks and olive trees to another gate and a fork. At the left you will see a large marker stone, painted red, blue and yellow. This marks our *return* path, but for now

Sa Cova
de Ses Bruixes

Rafal de
Ariant
153

N
1km

Mortitx
350

Pollensa

K11   K10

Lluc

© 1987 SUNFLOWER BOOKS

we go straight on — only to find that our path disappears. Head across open fields straight towards the coast — the lowest point on the horizon. The terrain becomes more and more rocky, till we come to a place where low stone walls meet *to form a right angle* (**40min**). Go through the gate and continue along the rocky path (sporadically marked with yellow dots). First it climbs; when it later descends, it's tougher going, because the path is not easily discernible.

At about **1h** turn up right 90°, by a rock with a horizontal red bar, following small rock-pile markers. Then at **1h10min** bear right 90° again, by a red-painted rock. As you climb the rocky slope, you might like to turn round for a view of the impressive landscapes behind you, with the Puig Tomir (Walk 14) high on the western horizon. Black vultures are often seen circling in this area. By about **1h20min**, you'll be able to glimpse the sea; then this old *senda* dips down and crosses a flattish area. Go through an opening in an old stone wall and, a little later, continue along the path that bends to the left. (The way to the right is blocked by a pile of rocks.) The route now winds down an impressive cliffside to the abandoned houses of Rafal de Ariant (under **2h**).

Wonderful rock formations along the C710 near Pollensa make for a dramatic — almost savage — landscape

From here it's only a short walk to the cliffs, perhaps with a goshawk or two circling overhead. The sea beats furiously on the rocks on a windy day. To see the Cova de Ses Bruixes, cross the plain from the house, bearing right, where a path leads down to the sea. Leaving this path, near a large boulder, follow on *very carefully* across the rocky slope to a stony platform, from where you will see the magnificent cave in the steep cliffside to the left. Its name means 'the witches' cave' in Mallorquin. This excursion takes about 20min from the house.

To return to Mortitx by the river bed — the *torrente* — take the path which runs down alongside the low stone wall, just near the house to the right, passing by some almond and fig trees, to where the stream bed lies between the huge rocks. You should only attempt this route back if the bed is dry, and it hasn't rained recently.

Follow the stream bed up through its rugged and beautiful valley, over rocks and boulders. At the first fork, turn to the right. Now the route becomes more difficult: you'll have to clamber over large, smooth rocks and boulders, and it can be quite dangerous if they are wet and slippery. Later the *torrente* passes through high and narrow clefts, between huge rocky cliffs. At the second fork, take the left-hand turning, and now the route becomes somewhat easier. Eventually we cross the main path, just below the houses of Mortitx (5h).

While it's always more enjoyable to return by a different route, it's more sensible to go back to Mortitx the way we came. The return is a bit faster past the point where the low walls meet: follow the rocky path marked with red paint (only easily seen from this direction), until you reach the colourful marker stone; here turn right for Mortitx (4h).

17 POLLENSA · THE TERNELLES VALLEY · EL CASTELL DEL REI · POLLENSA

IMPORTANT NOTE: The March family owns the Ternelles lands and they are only allowing walkers through on Mondays and only with a pass. The pass (good only on day of issue) must be obtained before 10am on Monday at the Banco March in Pollensa

Distance: 14km/8½mi; under 5h

Grade: easy to Ternelles; climb of 400m/1300ft on good track beyond

Equipment: stout shoes, sunhat, picnic, water; in winter, anorak and headscarf

How to get there: 🚌 to Pollensa; see also **STOP PRESS**, page 136
Depart Palma at: 10.00, 13.30, 17.30, 19.15 weekdays; departures at 10.00, 16.30, 20.30 Sundays and holidays; journey time 1 hour
To return: 🚌 from Pollensa to Palma
Depart Pollensa: 07.30, 09.15, 14.15, 17.45 weekdays; departures at 08.15, 15.00, 19.00 Sundays and holidays; journey time 1 hour

Short walk: Pollensa to the Ternelles stream *and return* (**A→B→A:** 6km/3½mi; 2h). Easy, on good track; equipment as above

---

This easy walk through the beautiful oak-shaded valley of the Ternelles river leads you up to the bleak coastal mountains and to the ancient ruins of a thirteenth-century castle. The walk can be made at any time of the year, since there's sufficient shade in the wooded valley — but put on your sunhat for the final stretch — a climb in full sun.

Leave the bus in the Calle Marques Destrull and **start the walk:** use the map on page 111 to follow the main street, through the Plaza Mayor and the smaller plaza with a fountain surmounted by a cockerel (the 'Fuente del Gallo'). The Calle Montesión and the Calle de la Huerta will then lead you to the bridge over the Torrente de San Jordi. From here you can see the old Roman bridge over to the right (**20min**). Cross the main Lluc—Pollensa road (C710) carefully and take the road straight ahead of you, signposted to Ternelles. This is a narrow tarmac country lane which winds its way through *possesiós* or

Water still flows in the old stone canaleta in the Ternelles Valley (Picnic 17)

fincas, through small cultivated areas and farm houses, populated with olive and fig trees.

Continuing along, you will soon (**40min**) see a modern *canaleta* going under a small stone bridge, and, immediately beyond, round the corner, look up to see a most original balcony on an old house on your right — it's made from the large wooden screws taken from an old olive press. Continuing along, you'll have an old stone wall (which still carries water in a channel at the top) on your right. Ignore the path to the left, which is private property, and keep discovering the valley of evergreen oaks and the Torrente de Ternelles. At **50min** you'll pass some water deposits on the right — storage for Pollensa. Just past here, you can see the Serra de Cornavaca up right. Looking down into the stream on the left, you'll spot the *canaleta* which used to carry water to Pollensa (see page 109).

The peaceful and shady Ternelles stream (Picnic 17)

Here you are now, in the valley, the Estret (Narrows) of Ternelles. At **55min** the large gates of the farm confront you. Produce your hard-won pass and through you go, to find a flat earthen track shaded by oaks. After a minute or two the fountain of Ternelles peeps out at you from its hiding place amongst the trees on the right. Walking through beautiful shady glades, occasionally hearing the tinkling of sheep bells, ignore the *camino forrestal* across the stream on your left, where there are stepping stones. This is one nice place to picnic and call a halt to the short walk.

Or continue a bit further by passing through the green gates straight ahead of you (*not* the gates to the farm on the left). If they are locked, go through the wooden access gate to the left, and continue along this pretty woodland walk, perhaps picnicking just past the gates, to end the short walk.

At **1h15min** go through more gates, over the bars which stop animals from wandering, and later take the signposted track up to the right (the way to the left leads to an old *ermita*, La Celda (The Cell). The route now leads on upwards, and you'll soon pass the remains of an old burnt limestone oven (see page 129) to the right. After a steady ascent, as you clear the trees, you will be able to see the large rocky clifftop in the distance.

The castle doesn't look very impressive yet, but wait and see! At under **2h** you'll come to a fork. Turn up left for the castle. (The continuing track leads on for some 5km down as far as the coast at Cala Castell.) It takes about thirty minutes to reach the castle. This impressive fortress was an important stronghold in Moorish times, and later, after the Spanish conquest. The views along the rugged northern coast are splendid. Cala Castell and Cala Estremer lie way below you, and the Serra del Cavall Bernat, just past Cala San Vicente, and the rocky Formentor cliffs can also be seen. There is something rather desolate about the bleak mountains along this uninhabited stretch of coastline, especially in winter. It must have been a lonely and chilly, windswept existence for the inhabitants of this stronghold, especially on a dark, stormy winter's night.

N

0   2km

© 1987 SUNFLOWER BOOKS

Puig de
S'Aguila
B
19
P
Hotel
Don Pedro
A

Cala Castell

CALA SAN
VICENTE

78
Coll de
Siller

544
Cornavaca

Castell
del Rei
476

SERRA DE CORNAVACA

220

La
Celda
17

Ternelles
P
Estret de Ternelles

100
B
Torrente de Ternelles

de

Torrente

70
A   17

18

Pe
Puig de María
333
A
K51,9
B

POLLENSA   111

Lluc

Inca

18 THE PUIG DE MARIA

See map pages 112-3
Distance: 3.5km/ 2mi; 1¼h
Grade: easy, but the ascent is 270m/885ft
Equipment: sunhat, stout shoes, picnic

Pollensa from the Puig de María (Picnic 18). The cypress-lined Calvary is clearly visible

How to get there: See Walk 17, page 109, for Pollensa bus details; ask to be put off at the Puig de María (pugj day Mah-ree-ah), on the PM220 just opposite the town of Pollensa

Short walk: as far up the *puig* as you like; there are good views after only 25min ascent (**A→B→A**: 1.8km/1mi; 40min *return*)

Opposite the town of Pollensa, a high, roundish mountain, the Puig de María, commands excellent views of the bays and the plain. The walk starts on the east side of the PM220, by the K51.9 marker (see town plan on page 111). The small country lane winds up through almond trees, towards the few small chalets built on the hillside. At the first bend, take the turning to the right, where blackberry bushes sprawl along the walls, and pass by the big, shady carob tree on the right. About five minutes along, take the bend up to the left (not straight on, where the road disappears), and continue winding up between the pretty houses with their flowering terraces.

Soon the route is shaded by pine trees and tall oaks, making this ascent pleasantly cool, refreshed by sea breezes. At about **25min**, the path rounds the side of the mountain, from where you will have superb views of Alcudia and its bay. Soon the centuries-old footpath is narrow and stoney. A small path leads off left at about **40min**. This narrow way leads to a small open area, where legend claims that the Virgin appeared to three women. Five minutes later, you'll arrive at the top, by the Ermita de la Mare de Deu (see pages 59 and 128). Unpack your picnic and enjoy the views!

See map on pages 112-113; see photograph opposite

Distance: 6km/3¾mi; under 2½h   Grade: easy climbs

Equipment: stout shoes, sunhat, picnic, water, anorak on cool days; long trousers, swimsuit, towel, suncream

How to get there: see bus timetables (p131) for Puerto de Pollensa; ask for 'Apartamentos Gommar'; return from Cala San Vicente by bus

Short walk: Hotel Don Pedro (**A**) as far as you like up Eagle Mountain (**B**); easy. Bus to Cala San Vicente; follow notes last paragraph

---

For some magnificent views of the rugged Formentor coastline, **start today's walk** at the Gommar apartments (map page 113). Follow the tarmac road opposite, and then the sandy track, as far as the old Finca Siller. (You may see loose guard dogs here; a stick is a wise precaution.) The track ends at the farm, but, just before the house, on the left, you will see a low brick wall between two hutches. Climb over the wall, to find yourself in the woods, where a quite easily seen trail leads on, towards the right. Go as far as the electricity pylons; then take the wider, stony path leading up left. In **25min** you'll come to a walled-in electricity plant on the hillside. Here turn sharp left in front of the walls, up the narrow, overgrown path through rocks and long grasses, marked at the outset by a large arrow made of loose stones on the ground. This winding path climbs to the low stone wall on the hillside, and follows up alongside it, coming out onto a track at about **35min**. Turn left again here, towards the white building belonging to the water board. About 100m (yds) past this building, another arrow of stones, again at ground level, indicates a left turn on a narrow path (the track leads over the hill to some houses). The path widens out and passes some chalets on its way to the cove (**45min**). If you swim, *beware of the undertow!*

Now let's explore the other side of the *cala*. Take the steps up and over to the other (northern) beach. From here follow the main road past the Hotel Don Pedro, until you come to a large house with a landscaped garden (200m/yds). Turn right on the track beside the garden walls. At the fork, turn right again to pass through iron gates. From here follow the easy track for half an hour, until it ends by a cave at the right (**1½h**). *Experienced* walkers can scramble up over the pink, marble rock to the summit, but *beware of the two very deep holes* dropping down to the cave (see also Walk 21). From the Aguila (Eagle) mountain you'll have fabulous views of the *calas* and the cliff-tops of the Reial, where the ruins of Castell del Rei (Walk 17) tower over an indigo sea.

Left: Pink marble-like rock and rosemary atop Mt Eagle (Picnic 19)

20 PUERTO DE POLLENSA · BOQUER VALLEY

See map on pages 112-113
Distance: 6 km/3¾ mi; 2¼ h   Grade: easy; gentle ascents/descents
Equipment/How to get there: as Walk 19; bus *into* Puerto de Pollensa
Short walk: Boquer Valley overlook and return (C→D→C: 3 km/
1¾ mi; 1¼ h); easy. Take sunhat, picnic, water; wear stout shoes

A very popular spot for bird-watchers, the long, wide Boquer valley reaches down to a lonely cove, where the elements venge their fury upon the rocks in winter, and the wind howls fiercely through, imprisoned by the jagged peaks of the Cavall Bernat to the north and the lower, bare mountains to the south that protect the Port of Pollensa.

Start out by heading for Formentor (signposted) on the main road. Turn left some 100 m (yds) past the Bec-Fi Restaurant. You'll see the Boquer Farm ahead on a ridge and pass the house in **25 min**. Go through a gate; then turn up right towards the old wooden gate. Beyond it lies the Boquer Valley, silent and peaceful, save for the bleating of goats. The solitary stand of pines shown below is reached in **35 min**; it's an ideal picnic spot and end to a short walk (**D**).

At **45 min** pass an old well (dry in summer) and continue along the right-hand side of the valley — the path finding its way through gaps in the old stone walls. Soon you'll glimpse the deep blue sea, and the enormous rock of Es Colomer, just off the rocky Formentor coastline. At **1h** come to a second natural water fountain, trickling into a stone trough. From here it's another ten minutes to the stony cove below.

Bird-watch from beneath these pines in the Boquer Valley (Picnic 20)

21 PUERTO DE POLLENSA · S'ATALAIA DE ALBERCUTX · CALA CALO

See map on pages 112-113

Distance: 10km/6mi; 3½h   **Grade:** easy, but many ups and downs!

Equipment/How to get there: as Walk 19; bus *into* Puerto de Pollensa
Taxi from Puerto de Pollensa to 'Mirador d'es Colomer'

Short walk: *mirador* parking place to Atalaya de Albercutx and
and return (E→F→E: 3km/1¾mi; 1¼h; fairly steep climb up a track;
take sunhat, picnic, water (headwear and warm clothing in winter).
Be sure to ask the driver to return for you (see 'Language hints', p63)

S 'Atalaia de Albercutx stands at 380m, overlooking the
incredibly beautiful bay of Formentor and its peninsula. **Our walk starts** at the steps to the fabulous Mirador
d'es Colomer, where there's likely to be a crowd of tourists.
Follow the track opposite the steps to the *mirador*, beside
a low brick wall. You'll round the hill, to find the tiny cove
of El Caló and Formentor coming into view. At about **25
min**, you'll see the entrance to a long, dark tunnel cut into
the mountainside, on your left: this was built just after the
Spanish Civil War, during World War II, and was meant for
storing arms and ammunition. Five minutes later, past an
old brick water cistern, you'll see a small path leading off
over the brow of the hill towards a radio transmitter. If you
decide to investigate here, be *extremely careful!* There are
holes in the ground that drop down into the tunnel! The
route leads past the old army barracks to the top — again,
take care at the *atalaya*; there is only a low, broken wall at
the top, and sometimes the wind here can be fierce.

Back on the PM221, turn left, descending to the K4 stone,
where a sandy track leads off left, just where the road bends
and is spanned by electricity wires (**1h45min**). Climb up
here, and pass by the side of a pylon, continuing straight
ahead; the narrow way will then descend the opposite side
of the hill. It's a rather narrow, overgrown and rocky path;
watch out for loose stones. It takes about twenty minutes
to reach the peaceful, secluded beach, where the only
sounds are the waves lapping the shore and the cries of gulls.
From here, allow a little over one hour to return to the port.

*The Atalaya de
Albercutx, just
opposite the fan-
tastic mirador on
the Formentor
Peninsula. Arms
were stored here
during the Civil
War. See also page
126. (Picnic 21)*

22 ERMITA DE LA VICTORIA · PEÑA ROJA · ATALAYA DE ALCUDIA · PLAYA DE COLL BAIX · ALCUDIA

Distance: 17km/10¼mi; under 6h

Grade: Quite strenuous climbing during the first half of the walk; easy walking during the latter half; all paths are good

Equipment: stout shoes, sunhat, picnic, water, anorak

How to get there: 🚌 to Alcudia
Depart Palma 09.45; arrive Alcudia 10.45
Taxi (see 🚕 symbol on plan below) to the Ermita de la Victoria
To return: 🚌 from Alcudia *or* Puerto de Pollensa to Palma (see last paragraph of text on page 120)
Depart Alcudia 18.15; arrive Palma 19.30 daily *summer only*
Depart Puerto de Pollensa 17.30; arrive Palma 18.45 weekdays; departs Puerto de Pollensa 18.45 Sundays and holidays

Short walk: Ermita de la Victoria to Peña Roja *and return* (A→B→A: 3.5km/2mi; 1½h). Fairly strenuous climb of 400m/1300ft; equipment as above. Taxi to the Ermita and ask him to return for you in time for your bus (see timetables pp 130-2 and 'Language hints' p63)

Turquoise, royal blue, pale and deep green — these are just some of the shades of the sea along the beautiful, rocky coastline on the Aucanada peninsula. Contrasting with the deep green of the pines, and the sandy-coloured cliffs, this is an artist's paradise of colour. The best time for this outing is early on in the year, on a clear sunny day when the cold air sparkles and visibility is good. Or in

Picnic 22 — chose from Victoria Park (above) or the path to Peña Roja

the springtime, when a pleasant sea breeze cools the effects of the Mallorcan sun.

Leave the bus in Alcudia and find a taxi to take you to 'Ermita de la Victoria', where **the walk begins**. The track you want starts behind the old *ermita*, opposite the car park. Follow the wide and comfortable track as it climbs (quite steeply), taking in all the wonders of the views and breathing deep lungfulls of pine-scented air. At **20min** the track takes a sharp turn to the right: just beyond, you will see the small narrow path leading up to the Peña Roja, signposted by ICONA. This delightful little route takes you alongside the mountain, rounding the cliffs, following the coastline right along the headland, as far as the old *atalaya*, from where there are magnificent views of the Bay of Pollensa and the Formentor headland — a delightful place to end your short walk with a picnic by the old stone refuge, once used by the *atalaya* watchmen. The beautiful Cape of Pines lies below you, surrounded by the many-hued coastal waters — a colourful picture postcard.

Those making the long walk will return to the main track (**1h30min**) and continue along, rounding the Puig de Romany. A protective wooden fence allays feelings of vertigo as you climb towards the Atalaya de Alcudia on the now rocky path, looking out over the sea towards Menorca. In **2h** walking you will attain the highest point in the walk, when you reach this *atalaya*. The splendid panorama from here is indescribably beautiful, and a good part of the island may be seen. The impressive Cordillera lies to the right, with the plain below. Then following round, find the landscapes of so many of our island walks: the *puigs* — Mayor, Massanella, Tomir; the headlands of Pollensa, the mountains of Artá. Below, near the Alcudia beaches, the marshes of the Albufera glisten under the sun.

Returning from the *atalaya*, take the right-hand path, leading to the Playa de Coll Baix, a beautifully rugged, unspoilt beach between the cliffs. During the winding descent you'll see the small islet of Aucanada and its lighthouse. You'll have a splendid view of the beach from a high rocky pinnacle and, fifteen minutes later (**3h**), you'll come to an ICONA shelter — a welcome sight with its wooden tables and benches, and drinking fountain. This is an ideal spot for a picnic, in the shade, with the sound of the rollers breaking below. (As an alternative you could go down to the beach itself; this takes about 15 minutes. But remember that there's little shade and swimming is not recommended — there's a very strong undertow. The last lap of the path to the beach involves clambering over slippery rocks and boulders; be careful. Allow 20 minutes to climb back up.)

One hour after leaving the shelter at Coll Baix (**4h45min**) you'll arrive at some double iron gates, which mark the end of the Mount Victoria Park. You will find yourself on a narrow tarmac country road which will lead you back to the Bodega del Sol bar at the crossroads, opposite the Bar Ca'n Tomeu, in about half an hour (**5h15min**).

From here it's another 2km, or about 45 minutes on foot to Alcudia. If you've shortened the long walk (perhaps by omitting the climb to Peña Roja, or the decent to the beach at Coll Baix), you may have time to walk into the village and catch the *summer* 18.15 bus (in winter, the departure is too early — 14.15). Alternatively, you can ask at the bar for a taxi to be called, to take you to Alcudia — or to Puerto de Pollensa, for the later bus departure.

23 BETLEM · ES CALO · BETLEM

Distance: 4.5km/2¾mi; 1¾h

Grade: easy

Equipment/How to get there: as Walk 24 (page 122), but ask taxi driver to take you (and collect you from) Betlem

Short walk: Betlem to the abandoned house and return (A→B→A: 2km/1¼mi; 40min); easy

An exhilarating stroll, characterised by the sound of rollers breaking below on the rocks and the tangy scent of pines. From the Colonia de San Pedro, continue in your transport along the tarmac road, as far as the new summer residential area of Betlem, its sparkling white houses reminiscent of Binibeca on Menorca. Here's where **the walk starts.**

About 100m (yds) beyond the last chalet, the tarmac road ends, and a stony track begins (leave your car 20m up this track, if you're driving). Then follow on foot through some stone gate-posts, and start to meander along the coast. You'll soon have beautiful views of the wide bay of Alcudia: Ca'n Picafort is visible, and further on round the bay, the holiday resort of Alcudia and the Aucanada peninsula — all with the rocky Formentor headland as a background.

The walk alternates between open stretches and pines. Not long after setting out, Mount Morey towers high above on our right (561m/2840ft) — the highest point on the Artá range. At about **20min,** you'll come to a small abandoned house on the right — a good place to end the short walk with a picnic. There's a patio round the back, from where a path leads up behind the house, into the mountains.

Continuing along the track, it takes about an hour to reach the small bay of Es Caló, where one or two fishing craft bob gently up and down on the sheltered waters, protected from the heavy swell of the sea by a jetty.

Right: Mount Farruch, en route to Betlem. Below: the coast near Betlem (Picnic 23)

24 CALA MATZOCS · TORRE DE AUBARCA · PLAYA D'ES VERGER

Map page 124   Distance: 10km/6mi; under 3½h   Grade: easy
Equipment: stout shoes, sunhat, picnic, water, swimsuit, sun cream
How to get there: 🚌 to Artá (journey time 1½h)
Depart Palma 08.30 (Sun); dep 13.30 Mon—Sat; in *summer only*, also dep Palma 10.00 Mon—Sat. *Taxi to Cala Estreta and return to Artá*
NB: The Artá taxi rank (Calle Son Servera, 24) is on the other side of town from the bus stop (Avenida del Ferrocarril — C715). Telephone for a taxi from the Café Parisien (Tel: 562202). See 'Language hints', p63, to ask the driver to collect you for the return journey, no later than 30 minutes before bus departure time
To return: 🚌 from Artá to Palma (journey time 1½h)
Departs Artá 14.10 daily all year and 17.35 Mon—Sat all year
Short walk: Cala Estreta to the Torre de Aubarca and return (A→B→A: 2½km/1½mi; 1¼h); easy; equipment as above

The sea spray splashes over the bare rocks and stings your cheeks, as you stroll over the headlands along the rugged northern coastline of the Artá peninsula. Here there are numerous sandy beaches, far enough away from civilisation to be deserted, even in summer — and the Isle of Menorca can be seen floating on the horizon on a clear day. Yet there is a desolate air hanging over the mountains, a strange sadness about the hillsides, ravaged by multiple fires which have left only the writhing skeletons of once-majestic mountain pines.

By car or taxi make for Cala Estreta (see note and sketchmap on page 37). Here you'll see big open gates, the splendid entrance to an *urbanización* that was never built. Pass through, and keep to the left, turning left a few minutes later and driving down towards the sea. You'll see a sort of entrance gate on the right; here's where you leave your transport. The track we take begins just opposite, on the left-hand side of the road.

Start the walk along this track. You'll notice small palm bushes pushing up through the dry, sandy terrain (see photograph on page 106). This is one of the three main areas on the island where they grow; you'll also see them in the Boquer Valley and all around Pollensa. They gradually disappear in the mountains and then re-emerge in the south around Andraitx.

From the Torre de Aubarca there are splendid views over the northeast coastline (near Picnic 24)

The track forks in six minutes; keep left and it will give way to a path, just past some heaps of stones on the right. Soon the Faralló de Aubarca, a large rock jutting out of the sea, is seen — and the ancient Aubarca tower on the headland.

Let's go down to the first beach, at Cala Matzocs. We cross this pretty, sandy cove to the opposite side, where we see a recess in the rocks. The path continues up here and turns right, round the rocky headland — but don't go *too* far right, where the flaking rock might be dangerous. We then climb a slope (past a large rock with an 'A' on it), and continue along the coast, reaching the tower (under **40min**).

Now take the wide track that leads off directly in front of you, through still-surviving pines, and at **50min** pass through an old gate. At **1h10min** there are one or two forks in the track. Continue straight on and turn right a minute later where the track bends, following down towards the sea, with the salty tang of the wind. You'll soon arrive at the Playa de Font Celada (**1h25min**).

The track circles this beach and later rounds the rocky headland, keeping close to the coastline and passing by two solitary tamarind trees braving the sea spray on a windy day. Then we reach the beach at Cala Verger (**1h40min**), a nice place to picnic under the shade of pines, or on the beach.*

*It is possible to continue from here up to the *meseta*, where the track ends, and from there scramble to the Atalaya de Morey (3h return).

25 CALA RATJADA · CALA GUYA · COLL DE MARINA · CALA MESQUIDA

Distance: 7km/4¼mi; 2½h

Grade: easy ups and downs

Equipment: stout shoes, sunhat, picnic, swimwear, suncream

How to get there: to Cala Ratjada (journey time 2h)

Depart Palma 08.30 Sundays; depart 13.30 Mon—Sat. In *summer only*, there is an additional Mon—Sat departure at 10.00

To return: from Cala Ratjada to Palma (journey time 2h)

Departs 13.45 daily; also 17.05 Mon—Sat all year round

Short walk: Cala Ratjada to the Coll de Marina (A→B→A: 4.5km/ 2¾mi; 1¾h *return*); easy climb. May be combined with a scramble over the headland to the watchtower

· **See photo page 42**

Cala Verger

Playa de Font Celada

90

Torre de Aubarca

B 60

24

50

A

Artá

Cala Matzocs

Cala Estreta

0

N

© 1987 SUNFLOWER BOOKS

2km

Cala Mesquida

Cabo Freu

B

Coll de Marina
145

Jaumell
271

25

B

Es Guyó

Cala Guya

CALA RATJADA

N

Pasqual Marques

Plaza de los Pinos

Paseo Colon

CALA RATJADA

Artá 715

A

Cabo de Capdepera

A multitude of white sandy bays, bathed by turquoise lagoons, and bordered by deep green pine woods, awaits your discovery along the eastern coast of the island. Unfortunately, the groping tentacles of commercialism are also reaching into these paradisial hideaways, converting some of them into miniature concrete jungles, and such has been the sad fate of Cala Ratjada.

However, there is hope that the remaining untouched beaches will be preserved in their natural state, and so keep the ever-present threat of hotel construction at a distance.

Today's walk starts at the Plaza de los Pinos in Cala Ratjada, where we leave the bus. Walk east on the Calle Isaac Peral as far as the church; here turn left on the Calle Pascual Marques. This road leads right through to Cala Guya, reached in under **15min**.

Cala Guya is a beautiful, half-moon shaped bay, edged by sand dunes and bathed by a tranquil lagoon of pale blue and aquamarine waters, which has managed to retain some of its natural magic, in spite of the overflow of sun-seekers from neighbouring Cala Ratjada — although the beach here is sadly marred by large and ugly drinks kiosks in summer.

Let's go further afield. Walk right round the beach, to the northern end, past the 'sun-bed limit' signpost, towards the green garage doors in the trees. Go to the right of the garage doors, to find a small sandy track that continues ahead. (The track to the right leads out onto the small rocky headland of Es Guyó.)

Now we have a pleasant and easy hour's pine-shaded walk through the woods, over the Coll de Marina (145m/ 475ft). At **40min** pass by an old stone hut and go through an opening in the old stone wall. Ignore the small path to the right just beyond here, and other offshoots of the main track. When the track forks into two at **45min**, take the left fork, which leads up to the pass. A spot of red paint on a tree at **50min** indicates that you should continue on ahead ignoring the path to the left. Ten minutes later, pass by a low stone building in ruins. Soon the path begins to des-cend again towards the sea. Pass by a wide open space on the left, and at the fork, take the right-hand path, and then the left, following the way indicated by the stone arrows on the ground.

In **1h15min** you'll arrive at Cala Mesquida, where you can make your way down to the beach by going through the gap in the broken old wall, or you might decide to explore the heights. The lonely surrounding hillsides, and the rugged headland where the *atalaya* still searches the horizon for pirate ships, make other good picnic spots.

Atalayas

The *atalayas* are ancient watchtowers, built in the latter half of the sixteenth century, to guard against the frequent attacks of pirates and the ever-growing menace of invasion by the Turks.

More than thirty of these *atalayas* were in action in the year 1595, and much of the credit for their strategic siting is due to the magnificent work of Juan Binimelis — an astrologer, mathematician, doctor, priest and chronicler. His vast knowledge of the terrain, of topography, of artillery and of engineering made it possible to raise these stone outposts at the most suitable points. At the same time, other means of defence — such as La Torre in the Port of Alcudia and La Fortaleza de Albercutx — were in the planning stages.

From these high points of vigilance (called *talaias de foc* or 'fire towers' in Mallorquín), approaching sea-craft could be seen at a great distance, and fire and smoke signals were relayed across the island, warning of the danger. Once the enemy was sighted, the coastal inhabitants would take refuge, while the alerted naval forces would immediately move to the threatened areas.

You will encounter these watchtowers all round the island, and you'll visit several of them if you make any of our island walks. But even if you only see Mallorca from a car or coach, you'll surely visit the Talaia de Ses Animes, just south of Banyalbufar, now a superb *mirador*.

Let's consider just one interesting example of this network of watchtowers in action: A relay of signals between the Atalaya de Albercutx on the Formentor Peninsula (Walk 21), the Atalaya de Alcudia and the *atalaya* at Peña Roja on the Cape of Pines (Walk 22) and the Atalaya de Morey and Torre de Aubarca in the Artá mountains (Walk 24), more than adequately covered the only northern routes of entry to the island — the bays of Pollensa and Alcudia.

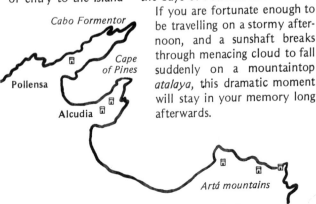

If you are fortunate enough to be travelling on a stormy afternoon, and a sunshaft breaks through menacing cloud to fall suddenly on a mountaintop *atalaya*, this dramatic moment will stay in your memory long afterwards.

Caça a coll

Thrushes are considered a great delicacy in Mallorca, and the *caça a coll* (thrush-netting) is a long-standing tradition on the Balearic Islands.

The thrushes arrive in late autumn and winter from colder countries, and are especially fond of olives, but are themselves prey for larger birds, such as falcons and kestrels. Thus the thrushes fly only at dusk and early morning — between the tops of the tall oaks where they take refuge at night and the lower olive orchards. They tend to glide between the trees, and not above them, so as to protect themselves from the keen eyes of the bigger birds of prey.

The islanders noticed these habits and long ago devised a method of catching the birds. This consists of thinning out linear 'passages' between the trees and spanning a huge net held on two canes across the end of the passage. The *caçador* waits silently, hidden behind a bush, and when the birds fly down towards the netting, he quickly folds it over, thus capturing his unfortunate victims.

Many restaurants on Mallorca include this delicacy on their menus — the most popular dish perhaps being *tordos con col*, or roast thrushes wrapped in cooked cabbage leaves. It can be quite delicious, if you can force yourself to stop thinking of the poor little creature migrating happily to the sun, only to land up in the cooking pot!

Canaletas

These 'little canals' — irrigation channels — may still be seen around the island. Made of stone, they carry water from springs down the hillsides to irrigate crops. Today, most of these delightful free-flowing water courses have been replaced by metal conduits, for reasons of sanitation and to prevent evaporation — a great loss for lovers of the landscape. The island's most famous *canaleta* is 7km long and runs between the Gorg Blau area and Mancor del Valle; its history is outlined on page 89. If you're lucky, you will be able to see a lovely *canaleta* in free flow if you make Walk 17, in the Ternelles Valley (see photograph page 109).

Casas de nieve

The *casas de nieve* (literally 'snow houses') are deep pits, only found on the highest part of the *sierra*. Here snow was stored to make ice before the advent of the refrigerator.

During the winter months, when heavy snow fell on the mountains, a group of men would set out for the peaks and fill these deep, stone-walled holes with snow, treading and packing it down hard. Once full, the pit was covered over with ashes or salt, and it remained frozen solid until the arrival of warmer weather. One man would stay behind, to tend the salt or ash covering, making repairs if necessary.

In summer, and at night, blocks of ice about fifty kilos (1 cwt) were loaded onto mules and taken down into the towns and villages, where they were used not only to make ice-creams and the like, but also for medicinal purposes. The so-called *oli de neu* (Mallorquín for 'snow-oil'), which was a mixture of ice and olive oil, was used to heal wounds and was reputed to stop bleeding.

There are many of these *casas de nieve* on the mountains of Massanella, Mayor, Teix and Tomir.

Ermitas

There are many *ermitas*, or sanctuaries, on Mallorca. Some of them are even today the homes of hermits who lead a simple and solitary life. Dressed in long brown wool habits, their long white beards and shaven heads remind us of mediaeval times.

Although much early evidence of hermit life has been discovered on the island, Ramon Llull is accepted by the Mallorcans as being the founder of *eremetismo*. Born a few years after the invasion of Mallorca by Jaime I in 1229, Llull was the son of a Catalán who accompanied the king during his conquest. Ramon Llull himself then became the steward of the future king, Jaime II, while still in his teens. Later, he married Blanca de Picany, by whom he had two children. As he grew older, however, he found that his Latin passions could not be satisfied solely by his wife, and he turned to other *amantes* in search of further pleasure and deeper fulfillment.

At about the age of thirty, he experienced a sudden conviction of his sins and turned to strict penitence — making pilgrimages to the sanctuaries of Santiago de Compostela and Montserrat. Back on Mallorca, in 1275 he went to Randa, living in a small grotto on the hillside. Later, he founded a missionary school in Valldemossa, where oriental languages were taught to friars who would later travel in Asia and Africa to convert the followers of Islam.

Ramon Llull was martyred in North Africa in 1315, stoned to death by Saracens. His remains were brought back to Mallorca by a group of Genovese merchants, and his relics were placed in the Church of San Francisco in Palma.

A typical day in the life of a hermit starts at 01.00, when he rises for the first prayers of the day. A second call to prayer comes at 06.00, followed by breakfast and manual labour assigned by the superior. After the main meal is eaten at 12.30, the afternoon and evening are spent in prayer, self-examination, meditation and further labour. Lights are out at 21.00, and each hermit retires to his cell where he rests until, at 01.00, the day repeats itself. A love of the solitary life is a must for all would-be monks!

The governing superior resides at the Sanctuary of San Salvador, near Felanitx (Tour 9), and is elected every six years by the hermits themselves. Novices begin their trial periods at the Ermita de Betlem near Artá (Tour 6).

Of special interest to lovers of the countryside (and walkers in particular) is the opportunity to stay overnight at various sanctuaries scattered around the island. The simple accommodation is spotless, and owing to the remote position of the *ermitas* on their hilltops, the overviews are always superb. See also page 59, 'Where to stay'.

Hornos de calç

You'll see the remains of many of these ovens (*hornos*) around Mallorca. They were used to produce lime (*calç*) for whitening the interiors of houses, or to be mixed with fine gravel for use in building.

The work was usually carried out by three men, working day and night for anything between nine and fifteen days. A great amount of heat was necessary to produce the reaction: $CaCO_3 \rightarrow CaO + CO_2$, and in these ovens an enormous quantity of wood was burned to obtain the heat required. Normally, the thinner logs which were not suitable for the charcoal industry (see *sitjas* below) were used, and any amount up to two tons could be burnt during one 'cooking'! Special stones, *piedra viva*, were used, and were usually found on the surrounding hillsides. A normal-sized oven would produce between a hundred and a hundred and fifty tons of burnt lime in one session.

Sitjas

Circular earth mounds, ringed with stones and now covered in moss — *sitjas* — are the only remains of the old charcoal industry. In summer months the charcoal makers lived with their families in the oak woods on the mountainsides. The sturdiest logs from the holm oak were used, and the fires burned round the clock — producing about one and a half tons of charcoal in a week — but the work was poorly paid. Sometimes the remains of a stone hut dwelling are to be found near the *sitjas* (see Picnic 12).

TRANSPORT TIMETABLES

Timetables are given on pages 131-132 for all the transport used to make the walks and picnics in this book. Use the alphabetical list of destinations below to find the appropriate timetable (note that 'Bus 1' means bus *timetable* 1 — not an actual bus number). Also included in the list below are some other departure times which you might find useful. Please remember that **changes to schedules are frequent**. Do not rely **solely** on these timetables, but get an up-to-date list from the Tourist Office or a tourist information kiosk near to your hotel. Also remember that while 'summer' generally means 1 May — 30 September, these dates are flexible — depending on weather conditions and how many tourists are about! It always pays to ask your hotel porter to 'phone to the transport company — or to go there yourself — to check the validity of whichever timetables you use — those in this book or even the ones from the Tourist Office! If you're staying outside Palma, enquire at your hotel to see if there are any useful local bus services in the area.

DESTINATION	departs from Palma			departs for Palma		
Alaró	see Train 1 (p132)					
Alcudia	see Bus 4 (p131)					
Andraitx	see Bus 5 (p131) and Bus 8 (p132)					
Artá	see Bus 1 (p131)					
Banyalbufar□	10.00			17.50*	18.35†	
Bunyola	see Train 2 (p132)					
Caimari	see Bus 3 (p131)					
Cala Bona	10.00	13.30	17.15	07.00	08.45	15.15
Cala d'Or	09.30	14.45	19.30	07.15	12.15	17.00
Cala Ratjada	. see Bus 1 (p131)					
Cala San Vicente○	10.00	13.30		13.45	18.00	
Calas de Mallorca	10.00	17.15		07.45	09.15	15.00
Campanet	09.00†	12.45*		14.45*	17.00†	19.00*
Ca'n Picafort	09.45	13.30	18.15	07.40	09.00	16.00
Colonia de San Jordi	19.30			07.50		
Deiá	see Bus 7 (p132)					
Escorca	see **STOP PRESS** (p136)					
Esporles	see Bus 2 (p131)					
Estellenchs□	10.00			17.30*	18.15†	
Felanitx	09.30	13.00	16.00	08.00	14.00	17.45
Inca	see Bus 3, Bus 4, Bus 6 (p131) and Train 1 (p132)					
La Puebla	13.30	18.15		08.00	14.45	
Lluc	see Bus 3 (p131); see also **STOP PRESS** (p136)					
Manacor	see Bus 1 (p131)					
Moscari	09.15	11.30	13.00	17.30	18.45	19.30
Muró	13.30	18.15		08.00	14.45	
Paguera	see Bus 5 (p131)					
Petra	09.30	13.00	16.30	07.30	14.25	17.50
Pollensa	see Bus 6 (p131) and **STOP PRESS** (p136)					
Porto Cristo	10.00	13.30	17.15	09.40	14.15	17.30
Porto Petro	14.45			16.30		
Puerto de Alcudia	see Bus 4 (p131)					
Puerto de Andraitx	see Bus 5 (p131)					
Puerto de Pollensa	see Bus 6 (p131) and **STOP PRESS** (p136)					
Puerto de Sóller	see Bus 7 and Tram (p132); see also **STOP PRESS** (p136)					
San Telmo	see Bus 8 (p132)					
Santa Eugenia	see Bus 9 (p132)					
Santa María	see Bus 6 (p131) and Train 1 (p132)					
Santanyí	09.30	14.45	19.30	07.50	12.50	17.30
Selva (see also Bus 3)	09.15	11.30	13.00	17.40	18.55	19.40
Ses Salines	09.30	14.45	19.30	07.45	13.05	17.40
Sóller	see Bus 7, Train 2, Tram (p132); also **STOP PRESS** (p136)					
Valldemossa	see Bus 7 (p132)					

□ summer only   * not Sundays/holidays
† only Sundays/holidays   ○ also departures from Pto. Pollensa

BUS 1
Palma — Manacor —
Artá — Cala Ratjada

	Monday – Saturday			Sundays/holidays
Palma	10.00□	13.30	17.15	19.45	08.30
Manacor	10.50□	14.20	18.05	20.35	09.20
Artá	11.30□	15.00	18.45	21.15	10.00
Cala Ratjada	12.00□	15.30	19.15	21.45	10.30
Cala Ratjada	07.30	13.45	17.05		13.45
Artá	08.00	14.10	17.35		14.10
Manacor	08.40	14.55	18.15		14.55
Palma	09.30	15.45	19.05		15.45

BUS 2
Palma — Esporles

WINTER (1 October – 30 May)
Monday – Friday

Palma	07.25	12.00	13.15	16.30	18.15	19.30
Esporles	07.55	12.30	13.45	17.00	18.45	20.00
Esporles	07.00	07.55	09.10	14.45	18.40	
Palma	07.30	08.25	09.40	15.15	19.10	

Saturdays

					Sundays/holidays	
Palma	09.00	13.00	15.30	19.30	10.00	15.30	19.30
Esporles	09.30	13.30	14.00	20.00	10.30	16.00	20.00
Esporles	08.20	09.30	15.00	17.30	08.30	15.00	18.30
Palma	08.50	10.00	15.30	18.00	09.00	15.30	19.00

SUMMER (1 June – 30 September)
Monday – Saturday

Palma	10.00	12.00	14.00	16.00	19.30	20.30
Esporles	10.30	12.30	14.30	16.30	20.00	21.00
Esporles	07.45	09.10	15.30	18.30		
Palma	08.15	09.40	16.00	19.00		

Sundays and holidays

Palma	10.00	16.00	20.00
Esporles	10.30	16.30	20.30
Esporles	09.10	15.30	19.15
Palma	09.40	16.00	19.45

BUS 3
Inca — Selva —
Caimari — Lluc
(connects with train from Palma)

Inca	09.45	17.00	Lluc	11.00	18.00
Selva	09.55	17.10	Caimari	11.15	18.15
Caimari	10.05	17.15	Selva	11.20	18.20
Lluc	10.20	17.35	Inca	11.30	18.30

BUS 4
Palma — Inca —
Alcudia — Puerto
de Alcudia

Palma	09.45	12.00	13.30	18.00	19.00□
Inca	10.00	12.15	13.45	18.15	19.15□
Alcudia	10.45	13.00	14.30	19.00	20.00□
Puerto de Alcudia	11.00	13.15	14.45	19.15	20.15□
Puerto de Alcudia	07.15	09.15	11.15	14.15	18.15□
Alcudia	07.30	09.30	11.30	14.30	18.30□
Inca	07.55	09.55	11.55	14.55	18.55□
Palma	08.30	10.30	12.30	15.30	19.30□

BUS 5
Palma — Paguera —
Andraitx — Puerto
de Andraitx

Frequent departures, too numerous to list. Approximate
journey times as follows: Palma — Paguera 40min; Paguera —
Andraitx 20min; Andraitx — Puerto de Andraitx 15min
WINTER: buses depart Palma daily at 07.10 and every 45min
thereafter until 19.30; depart Puerto de Andraitx 07.15 and
every 45 minutes thereafter until 19.30
SUMMER: more frequent buses, with departures at both
ends of the route at the following times
07.00 07.35 08.10 08.45 09.30 09.55 10.30 11.05
11.40 12.15 12.50 13.25 14.00 14.35 15.10 15.35
16.20 16.55 17.30 18.05 18.40 19.15 20.00

BUS 6
Palma — Santa María
— Inca — Pollensa —
Puerto de Pollensa

	Monday–Saturday			Sundays/holidays		
Palma	10.00	13.30	17.30	19.15	10.00	16.30	20.30
Santa María	10.20	13.50	17.50	19.35	10.20	16.50	20.50
Inca	10.40	14.10	18.10	19.55	10.40	17.10	21.10
Pollensa	11.00	14.30	18.30	20.15	11.00	17.30	21.30
Pto Pollensa	11.15	14.45	18.45	20.30	11.15	17.45	21.45
Pto Pollensa	07.15	09.00	14.00	17.30	08.00	14.45	18.45
Pollensa	07.30	09.15	14.15	17.45	08.15	15.00	19.00
Inca	07.50	09.35	14.35	18.05	08.35	15.20	19.20
Santa María	08.10	09.55	14.55	18.25	08.55	15.40	19.40
Palma	08.30	10.15	15.15	18.45	09.15	16.00	20.00

NB: All transport is daily unless otherwise coded

132   Landscapes of Mallorca

BUS 7
Palma — Valldemossa —Deiá—Sóller— Puerto de Sóller

WINTER (1 October – 30 March)

Palma	10.00	12.00*	15.00	19.00
Valldemossa	10.30	12.30*	15.30	19.30
Pto Sóller	10.45	12.45*	15.45	19.45
Deiá	11.15	13.15*	16.15	20.15

Deiá	07.30	15.00	17.30
Pto Sóller	08.00	15.30	18.00
Valldemossa	08.30	16.00	18.30
Palma	09.00	16.30	19.00

SUMMER (1 April – 30 September)

Palma	07.45	10.00	12.00*	16.30	20.00
Valldemossa	08.15	10.30	12.30*	17.00	20.30
Deiá	08.30	10.45	12.45*	17.15	20.45
Pto Sóller	09.00	11.15	13.15*	17.45	21.15

Pto Sóller	07.00	09.30	14.30	16.00*	18.30
Deiá	07.30	10.00	15.00	16.30*	19.00
Valldemossa	08.00	10.30	15.30	17.00*	19.30
Palma	08.30	11.00	16.00	17.30*	20.00

BUS 8
Palma — Andraitx — San Telmo

Palma	09.00†	San Telmo	17.15†
Andraitx	10.00†	Andraitx	17.45†
San Telmo	10.30†	Palma	18.45†

BUS 9
Palma — Santa María — Santa Eugenia

	Monday–Saturday			Sun/holidays	
Palma	13.30	19.00		09.00	19.00
Santa María	13.50	19.20		09.20	19.20
Santa Eugenia	14.05	19.35		09.35	19.35
Santa Eugenia	07.00	08.00	15.15	08.00	18.00
Santa María	07.10	08.10	15.25	08.10	18.10
Palma	07.35	08.35	15.50	08.35	18.35

TRAINS

TRAIN 1
Palma — Santa María — Alaró y Consell — Inca

Palma	06.00	and every hour until	21.00
Santa María	06.15		21.15
Alaró y Consell	06.25		21.25
Inca	06.35		21.35
Inca	06.00	and every hour until	21.00
Alaró y Consell	06.10		21.10
Santa María	06.20		21.20
Palma	06.35		21.35

TRAIN 2**
Palma — Bunyola — Sóller

Palma	08.00	10.40	13.00	15.15	19.45	22.00†
Bunyola	08.26	11.03	13.26	15.40	20.10	22.25†
Sóller	09.00	11.45	14.00	16.15	20.45	23.00†
Sóller	06.45	09.15	11.50	14.10	18.20	21.00†
Bunyola	07.15	09.45	12.15	14.35	18.45	21.25†
Palma	07.45	10.15	12.50	15.10	19.20	22.00†

TRAM
Sóller — Puerto de Sóller

Departures from Sóller

05.55	07.00	08.00	09.00	10.00	11.00	11.30	12.00
12.30	13.00	14.00	15.00	16.00	16.30	17.00	17.30
17.55	19.00	20.00	20.45				

Departures from Puerto de Sóller

06.20	07.30	08.25	09.30	10.30	11.30	12.00	12.30
13.00	13.25	14.30	15.30	16.30	17.00	17.30	17.55
18.30	19.30	20.20	21.10				

BOAT
Puerto de Sóller — La Calobra

Pto Sóller	10.30	11.30	15.00	*Sailings May– September (depending on weather)*
La Calobra	11.20	12.20	15.50	
La Calobra	14.00	15.00	16.45	
Pto Sóller	14.50	15.50	17.35	

**The Sóller–Pollensa bus meets the 08.00 train from Palma; however, on the return run it arrives at Sóller too late to catch the last Palma-bound train

□ summer only
* does not run Sundays/holidays
† Sundays/holidays only

Geographical names only are included here; for non-geographical entries, see Contents, page 3. A page number in *italic type* indicates a map reference; **bold type** indicates a photograph or sketch. "TM" refers to the map on the reverse of the fold-out touring map.

GLOSSARY

atalaya – watchtower
caça a coll – thrush-netting
caçador – hunter
camino – road, way
ca'n – contraction of the
    Mallorquín 'casa d'en' –
    'house of'
canaleta – irrigation channel
carrer – street (Mallorquín)
carretera – highway
casa de nieve – snow pit
coll – pass
coll de caçar – 'shooting pass';
    place for thrush-netting
comedero – feeding ground
cordillera – mountain range
coto privado de caça –
    private hunting ground
embalse – reservoir
ermita – hermitage

finca – farm
font – fountain, spring
fronton – pelota court
horno de calç – lime oven
parada – bus stop
pla – plain, tableland
planicie – plain, tableland
puig – mountain
rama – branch
romería – pilgrimage
senda – footpath, trail
serra – mountain range
    (Mallorquín)
sierra – mountain range
    (Spanish)
sitja – fireplace
son – 'estate of' (Mallorquín)
talayots – prehistoric stones
torrente – torrent or stream;
    Mallorca has *no* rivers

See pages 126–129 for more details

STOP PRESS

BUSES ON THE C710: There is only one bus a day, leaving Soller at 09.00 and returning from Puerto de Pollensa at 17.00. Until a morning bus from Pollensa is introduced, this is *not* a good centre from which to make mountain walks. But Lluc is quite well placed for Walks 13, 14, 16, 17-21. Otherwise, Soller and Puerto de Soller become, along with Palma, the best overnight centres for walkers. The current timetable is shown below.

Sóller	09.00	Pto Pollensa	17.00	*This service is*
Pto Sóller	09.30	Cala S Vicente	17.10	*daily in summer*
Ses Barques	09.45	Pollensa	17.20	*(approximately*
Son Torellas	10.05	Lluc	18.00	*Easter until end*
Escorca	10.20	Escorca	18.20	*September) and*
Lluc	10.35	Son Torellas	18.35	*weekends only*
Pollensa	11.20	Ses Barques	18.50	*in winter.*
Cala S Vicente	11.30	Pto Sóller	19.10	
Pto Pollensa	11.45	Sóller	19.25	

Page 67, WALK 2: in March 1987 this walk was impassable at about the halfway mark, due to a landslide.

Page 111, POLLENSA MAP: Note that the Soller–Pollensa bus stop is opposite the road to Ternelles, not in the Calle Marques Destrull (where the Palma–Pollensa bus stops).